BEGINNER'S HAWAIIAN

BEGINNER'S HAWAIIAN

ZELIE DUVAUCHELLE SHERWOOD

KU PA'A PUBLISHING INCORPORATED
AND PRESS PACIFICA, LTD.

FIFTH PRINTING 1996
FOURTH PRINTING 1994
THIRD PRINTING 1992
SECOND PRINTING 1989
FIRST PRINTING 1981

ISBN 0-914916-56-4 paperback

Manufactured in the United States of America

Published by
KU PA'A PUBLISHING INCORPORATED
(formerly Topgallant Publishing Co., Ltd.) and
PRESS PACIFICA, LTD.
PO Box 37460
Honolulu, Hawaii 96837

DEDICATION

Dedicated to the memory of my maternal
grandmother, PUAALA, my father
EDWARD KEKUHI DUVAUCHELLE
and my paternal grandmother KUKU MELE,
who taught me to love the old Hawaii,
the old Hawaiian way of living
as well as to speak the Hawaiian language fluently.

To My Grandmother
PUAALA

I owe my knowledge of Hawaiian. She gave me my foundation at a very early age. It was she who carefully trained and drilled me daily in reading, writing and speaking Hawaiian. In addition to this I had to read to her the *Kuokoa* and *Alohaaina,* two Hawaiian newspapers, two hours each Saturday and occasionally to translate into Hawaiian, English letters that I received from home while living with her.

PREFACE

In preparing this book, I have endeavored to make it useful and practical. I have also endeavored to construct a method by uniting, in a clear and concise manner, all that is essential to acquire, in the shortest possible time, a practical and correct knowledge of the Hawaiian language.

It is my intention to make this grammar interesting, colorful and stimulating by avoiding rules that tend to confuse the student. However, I do not wish to teach solely through conversational Hawaiian wherein the student commits to memory phrases and sentences, repeated parrot-like, with only a limited understanding of the language and little knowledge of sentence structure. I prefer to stress sufficient grammar to give the student ability to express his thoughts accurately.

To be able to read the Hawaiian language correctly is an accomplishment; however, to speak it correctly and with thorough understanding is indeed an achievement.

My aim is to show those who wish to study the language a method which will meet the general requirement, be worth learning and, at the same time, avoid long and tedious effort which will be of little value.

A Service Station and repair shop in Kaunakakai.

CONTENTS

FOREWORD

This book is intended to provide a practical teaching manual in the Hawaiian language. The contents deal with the basic fundamentals of the language, beginning with the alphabet, the proper pronunciation, and concentrating on drills and exercises. The aim has been to make the language easy to learn and, once learned, not quickly forgotten.

It deals with some explanations on different types of verbs and examples of the proper way to use them in sentences. It also deals with the possessive pronouns and their uses in making sentences, as well as their use in expressing the verb "to be" and the verb "to have."

The general purpose of our study of Hawaiian grammar is to help the student not only to control the simple and familiar Hawaiian, but to remember it as well.

It is taken for granted that the student studying Hawaiian understands the principles of general grammar, hence many definitions and explanations have been omitted.

It may be well to state briefly how this textbook came to be written. In 1930, Mr. Lang F. Akana, then the president of the Hawaiian Civic Club, started me on my way. When he first discovered my knowledge of the Hawaiian language, he invited me to speak to the Hawaiian Civic Club at several of their luncheon meetings. He encouraged me to continue my research in the language and culture of old Hawaii, which stimulated me to gather material for the purpose of instructing in Hawaiian.

In 1938, I taught my first class in Hawaiian language. In 1955, I wrote my first Hawaiian grammar.

The author's father and mother with their fourteen children.

The author's home taken from across Pukoo fish pond, 1924.

The author's father with his three brothers.

The author's aunt and cousin, sisters and brother, 1924.

The author's kuke mele, paternal grandmother, holding the author's brother Gene.

The author's father and mother, sister Louise and nephew Jackie Goodhue.

The suspension bridge in Halawa, Ka uapo holuholu o Halawa.

INTRODUCTION

1. PRONUNCIATION

A clear table of Hawaiian sounds with their nearest equivalent in English is given below. The student can master these sounds easily in a few drills, learning several each day with an experienced Hawaiian instructor, if possible. He should then be able to pronounce any word at sight.

This method of acquiring pronunciation is far superior to the practice of committing to memory the phonetic pronunciation of words.

2. ALPHABET

The true Hawaiian alphabet consists of but twelve letters — five vowels and seven consonants. They are recited in this order; first the vowels then the consonants.

Vowels	Consonants
A - (ah)	H - (hay)
E - (eh)	K - (kay)
I - (ee)	L - (lah)
O - (oh)	M - (moo)
U - (ooh)	N - (noo)
	P - (pee)
	W - (vay)

Alphabet Ditty

A alapii	A	alapii means a stairway
E elepani o kai	E	elepani o kai means elephant of the sea (walrus)
I ipuhao keleawe	I	ipuhao keleawe is an iron pot
O oo mahiai	O	oo is a spade to farm with
U upa makani	U	upa makani means bellows
H hoki	H	hoki is a mule
K kao	K	kao is a goat
L liona	L	liona is a lion
M muumuu	M	muumuu is a loose gown
N nuhou	N	nuhou means news
P peahi	P	peahi is a fan
W waiwai nui	W	waiwai nui means great wealth

3. VOWEL SOUNDS

Vowel sounds are generally uniform with some exceptions as illustrated below.

A has the sound of **ah,** as in far, tar.
Sometimes *A* has the sound similar to the English **uh,** as:
make (muk'-ky) not (mah'-kay).
male (mul'ley) not (mah'-lay).

E has the sound of **ay** in bay, lay.
E also has a shorter sound, as
Nele (nel'-ly) not (nay'-lay).
Pele (pel'-ly) not (pay'-lay).

I has the sound of **e** in Eva, or the sound of **i** in ink.

O has the sound of **o** in no, so;
Never the sound of o in nose, pose, which to a Hawaiian has the sound of "ou."

U has the sound of **oo** in too, moo, or the sound of **u** in true, blue; never the sound of u in mule, use, which to a Hawaiian has the sound "iu."

Exercise in Pronunciation

A	E	I	O	U
E	I	O	U	A
I	O	U	A	E
O	U	A	E	I
U	A	E	I	O

4. VOWEL COMBINATIONS

All vowels in Hawaiian are pronounced. There are no silent letters. Each vowel has but one sound and no two vowels are ever combined to make one sound as in the English words brought, taught, cook, seek. Thus we say that there are no improper diphthongs in the Hawaiian language.

The sound of the English vowels, the long "a," "i", "o" or "u" and the short "i" as a Hawaiian hears it, would each have the sound of two different vowels following each other, as follows:

a in ate would be written *ei.*
i in high and y in my would be written *ae.*
i in kite would be written *ai.*
o in nose would be written *ou,* and
u in mute would be written *iu.*

When two or more of the same vowels follow each other in the same word, each vowel is pronounced with a distinct break between them.

Examples:

aa is pronounced **ah'-ah**
ee is pronounced **eh'-eh**
ii is pronounced **ih'-ih**
oo is pronounced **oh'-oh**
uu is pronounced **ooh'-ooh**
aaa is pronounced **ah-ah'-ah**
eee is pronounced **eh-eh'-eh**
iii is pronounced **ih-ih'-ih**
ooo is pronounced **oh-oh'-oh**
uuu is pronounced **ooh-ooh'-ooh**

When there are two or more different vowels together in the same word, each vowel is pronounced distinctly and separately. Yet, they are often united to make one continuous sound, as *palaoa* (pronounced somewhat like the English word flour).

Examples:

ae, ai, ao, au, ea, ei, eo, eu, ia, ie, io, iu, oa, oe, oi, ou, ua, ue, ui, uo.

> *ae* is pronounced like **i** in high
> *ai* is pronounced like **i** in light
> *ao* is pronounced like **ow** in how
> *au* is pronounced like **ou** in ouch
> *ea* is pronounced **eh'-ya**
> *ei* is pronounced like **a** in ate
> *eo* is pronounced like **ayo** in bayonet
> *eu* is pronounced **eh'-yoo**
> *ia* is pronounced **ee'-ya**
> *ie* is pronounced like **ye** in yet
> *io* is pronounced like **yo** in yodel
> *iu* is pronounced **ih'-yoo**
> *oa* is pronounced **oh'-wah**
> *oe* is pronounced **oh'-weh**
> *oi* is pronounced **oh'-wih**
> *ou* is pronounced like **o** in nose
> *ua* is pronounced **ooh'-wah**
> *ue* is pronounced **ooh'-weh**
> *ui* is pronounced **ooh'-wih**
> *uo* is pronounced **ooh'-woh**

5. GLOTTAL STOPS BETWEEN VOWELS

There are glottal stops between two or more different vowels following each other in the same word. This occurs when there is a distinct stop or catch of the breath. It is represented by a reverse apostrophe between the vowels as *aʻo* (pronounced **ah'-oh**).

Examples:

a'e is pronounced **ah'-eh**	*i'o* is pronounced **ih'-oh**
a'i is pronounced **ah'-ih**	*i'u* is pronounced **ih'-ooh**
a'o is pronounced **ah'-oh**	*o'a* is pronounced **oh'-ah**
a'u is pronounced **ah'-ooh**	*o'e* is pronounced **oh'-eh**
e'a is pronounced **eh'-ah**	*o'i* is pronounced **oh'-ih**
e'i is pronounced **eh'-ih**	*o'u* is pronounced **oh'-ooh**
e'o is pronounced **eh'-oh**	*u'a* is pronounced **ooh'-ah**
e'u is pronounced **eh'-ooh**	*u'e* is pronounced **ooh'-eh**
i'a is pronounced **ih'-ah**	*u'i* is pronounced **ooh'-ih**
i'e is pronounced **ih'-eh**	*u'o* is pronounced **ooh'-oh**

Exercise in Pronunciation

aa	ae	a'e	ai	a'i
ao	a'o	au	a'u	a
ea	e'a	ee	ei	e'i
eo	e'o	eu	e'u	e
ia	i'a	ie	i'e	i
ii	io	i'o	iu	i'u
o	oa	o'a	oe	o'e
oi	o'i	oo	ou	o'u
u	ua	u'a	ue	u'e
ui	u'i	uo	u'o	uu

6. CONSONANTS

Most of the consonants are sounded as in English.

H has only the aspirate sound, K, L, M, N, and P have the same sounds as in English.

W resembles the English sound of **V.** It has the sound of the English W only when it follows one of the vowels "o" or "u" and, at the same time, precedes one of the vowels "a," "e" or "i." This combination must also appear in the last syllable to indicate that the accent follows the letter *W.*

Following are a few examples to illustrate this:

hua is pronounced **who'-wah**   *huwa* is pronounced **who-wah'**
oe is pronounced **oh'-weh**   *owe* is pronounced **oh-weh'**
ui is pronounced **ooh'-wih**   *uwi* is pronounced **ooh-wee'**
koa is pronounced **koh'-wah**   *kowa* is pronounced **koh-wah'**

The sound of the English W is made by a combination of the letter "u" followed by another vowel, such as William, written *Uilama* or *Uiliama;* watch, written *uaki;* wine, written *uaina;* but vine is written *waina.*

Exercise

ha	ka	la	ma	na	pa	wa
he	ke	le	me	ne	pe	we
hi	ki	li	mi	ni	pi	wi
ho	ko	lo	mo	no	po	wo
hu	ku	lu	mu	nu	pu	wu
haa	kaa	laa	maa	naa	paa	waa
hae	kae	lae	mae	nae	pae	wae
ha'e	ka'e	la'e	ma'e	na'e	pa'e	wa'e
hee	kee	lee	mee	nee	pee	wee
hei	kei	lei	mei	nei	pei	wei
he'i	ke'i	le'i	me'i	ne'i	pe'i	we'i
hii	kii	lii	mii	nii	pii	wii
hai	kai	lai	mai	nai	pai	wai
ha'i	ka'i	la'i	ma'i	na'i	pa'i	wa'i
hoo	koo	loo	moo	noo	poo	woo
hou	kou	lou	mou	nou	pou	wou
ho'u	ko'u	lo'u	mo'u	no'u	po'u	wo'u
huu	kuu	luu	muu	nuu	puu	wuu
hua	kua	lua	mua	nua	pua	wua
hu'a	ku'a	lu'a	mu'a	nu'a	pu'a	wu'a

7. SYLLABLES

A syllable in Hawaiian may consist of a single vowel, or a consonant united with a vowel or, at most, of a consonant and two vowels. It never contains more than one consonant.

Every syllable must end with a vowel and no syllable can have more than three letters; generally not more than two; and a great many syllables consist of but one vowel.

There are no unsounded or useless letters in the Hawaiian language.

Exercise

aha	aka	ala	ama	ana	apa	awa
ahi	aki	ali	ami	ani	api	awi
aho	ako	alo	amo	ano	apo	awo
ahu	aku	alu	amu	anu	apu	awu
eha	eka	ela	ema	ena	epa	ewa
ehu	eku	elu	emu	enu	epu	ewu
iho	iko	ilo	imo	ino	ipo	iwo
ihu	iku	ilu	imu	inu	ipu	iwu
ohi	oki	oli	omi	oni	opi	owi
uhi	uki	uli	umi	uni	upi	uwi

8. WORDS

Hawaiian words never end with a consonant nor ever have two consonants joined together. The only word that has ever been printed in Hawaiian books with two consonants together is *Kristo* (Christ) accepted in the Hawaiian language due to constant usage.

Many Hawaiian words imitate the sound of English pronunciation such as, *eka* (acre), *pipi* (beef), *puke* (book), *palaoa* (flour), *huila* (wheel).

In order to produce the Hawaiian pronunciation of English, Hawaiian letters are substituted for various consonants.

Examples:

P for b and f

baby - *pepe*	fever - *piwa*
bank - *panako*	France, French - *Palani*

K for c, d, g, j, q, s, t, x and z

cap - *kapu*	sabbath - *kapaki*
duck - *kaka*	telephone - *kelepona*
guava - *kuawa*	tin - *kini*
jelly - *kele*	xylophone - *kilopona*
queen - *kuini*	zebra - *kipala*

Exceptions to the rule are in proper names where *i* is used for j.

Jesus - *Iesu*	John - *Ioane* (from Juan)
Jacob - *Iakopa*	Joseph - *Iokepa*

Only the aspirate *h* is used in Hawaiian

ham - *hame*	heel - *hila*

L for r

rice - *laiki*	rabbit - *lapaki*

W for v

vinegar - *winika*	violin - *waiolina*
violet - *waioleka*	virgin - *wilikina*

U followed by another vowel for w

ware - *uea*	wick - *uiki*
Washington - *Uakinakona*	watch - *uaki*

H for wh

wheelbarrow - *huila palala*	whip - *huipa*
wheat - *huika*	whole - *holo*

I for y as in yard - *ia* (**eeh-yah'**)

Following the rules that every syllable must end with a vowel and that no Hawaiian word can have two consonants together, a vowel is added between consonants whenever needed.

Examples:

Candy - *Kanake*	George - *Keoki*
Johnny - *Keoni*	sailor - *kela* (**kel'-lah**)
	tailor - *kela* (**kel'-lah**)

The endings "ar," "er" and "or" in English words are pronounced *a* (**ah**) in Hawaiian.

cigar - *kika*	letter - *leka*
calendar - *kalana*	doctor - *kauka*
carpenter - *kamana'*	elevator - *eleweka*

However, the ending "or" in words like senator is pronounced *oa* (**oh'-wah**) as in senator - *kenakoa*.

Following are examples of some English words with their Hawaiian pronunciation.

bucket - *pakeke*	novel - *nowela*
candy - *kanake'*	owner - *ona*
deer - *kia*	pocket - *pakeke*
fig - *piku*	quart - *kuaka*
gallon - *kalani*	sailor* - *kelamoku*
hundred - *haneli*	tailor* - *kelalole*
jury - *kiule*	union - *uniona*
license - *laikini*	velvet - *weleweka*
market - *makeke*	zinc - *kini*

9. ACCENT

The accent is usually on the next to the last syllable. Occasionally it may be on the last syllable as shown in paragraph on consonants explaining the letter "W."

10. EUPHONY

Euphony is very important in Hawaiian. Word pronunciation should flow easily and without harsh sounds.

---

* Because the pronunciation of sailor and tailor are alike in Hawaiian, it is necessary to show some distinction between them; thus the words *moku* (boat) and *lole* (clothes) are added to the word *kela* to show the difference between sailor and tailor.

Exercise

aha	ahe	ahi	aho	ahu	epa
hae	ka'e	lae	mae	pae	wae
aka	ake	aki	ako	ala	ale
ha'i	la'i	mai	pa'i	kai	wai
alo	alu	ihe	ihi	iho	ihu
hao	ka'i	mao	ma'i	pau	waa
ike	iki	ena	ano	anu	ami
ila	ili	ilo	apa	apo	imi
hui	hu'i	hoa	hoe	ho'i	hua
imo	imu	awa	ina	ino	inu
hua	kua	lua	mua	nau	na'u
eha	ipu	eke	aku	eli	iwi
hoa	koa	loa	moa	noa	poo
ohe	ohi	ohu	emi	oki	ola

HAAWINA EKAHI
(Lesson One)

PRONOUNS
E aʻo Kakou i ka ʻolelo Hawaiʻi - Let us learn Hawaiian

In the Hawaiian language, as in English, pronouns are used in the place of nouns. In Hawaiian, however, they are also used for various other specific purposes, such as providing the means of expressing the verb "to be," the verb "to have" and the relative pronouns.

The accuracy of the language depends largely on the proper use of the pronouns. For this reason, they must be learned thoroughly and accurately.

There are four kinds of pronouns: Personal, possessive, demonstrative and interrogative.

There are no relative pronouns. However, the use of some personal and possessive pronouns in certain sentence structures expresses the relative pronouns.

Pronouns are in the first, second and third persons and have three numbers; singular (one person), dual (two persons) and plural (more than two persons).

They have no distinction of gender nor do they express neuter gender.

The Hawaiian language has two simple words, *ala* (there) and *nei* (here) which are very often used with the pronouns in the third person. We shall call them articles of location. They indicate location and are opposed to each other in meaning.

Ala means there, over there, in that place — away from the person speaking (illus. #1).

Nei means here, over here, in this place — in the possession of or near the person speaking (illus. #2).

Nei designates present place and time, here and now, while *ala* denotes distance in place only; i.e., it is correct to say "Hawaii *nei*" only when you are in Hawaii because it means here in Hawaii.

Referring to Hawaii from a location other than Hawaii, you must say "Hawaii *ala*," meaning there in Hawaii, over there in Hawaii.

Illus. #1: *Ke kahea ala kela keiki i kela wahine ala.*
That boy is calling to that woman over there.

Illus. #2: *Ke kii mai nei ke kanaka i keia keiki nei.*
The man is coming to get this boy over here.

HAAWINA ELUA
(Lesson Two)

Aloha, ea! - Greetings!
Ae, ke aloha no! - Yes, greetings!

PERSONAL PRONOUNS
Nominative Case

Singular
1st Person *au, owau** - I
2nd Person *oe* - you
3rd Person *oia* - he, she
> Note: *Oia* is the "o emphatic" prefixed to the pronoun *ia* of the third person.

3rd Person *oiala* - he (over there), or she (over there)
3rd Person *oinei* - he (over here), or she (over here)
> Note: When *ala* or *nei* is used in the third person singular, the *a* in *oia* is dropped and the words become *oiala* and *oinei*.

---

* *Owau* is the "o emphatic" prefixed to the pronoun *au* with the letter "w" inserted for euphony.

Dual (Two)
1st Person *kaua* - we (you and I)
1st Person *maua* - we (he and I, or she and I)
2nd Person *olua* - you (two)
3rd Person *laua* - they (two)
3rd Person *laua ala* - they (two over there)
3rd Person *laua nei* - they (two over here)

The first person dual has two forms.

The first form, *kaua,* implies that I include myself and the person I address, thus you and I.

E himeni kaua - let us (you and I) sing.

The second form, *maua,* implies that I speak of myself and one other person, excluding the person addressed.

E himeni ana maua - we (he and I or she and I) are singing. The person addressed is not included.

It should be stressed here that the correct usage of the dual number in Hawaiian is most rigidly adhered to, both in conversation and in writing. The dual and plural numbers are never interchanged. One never uses a dual number for a plural or vice versa.

Plural (More than two)

1st Person *Kakou* - We	you, they and I
	you, he and I
	you, she and I
1st Person *Makou* - We	he, she and I
	they and I
	she, they and I
	he, they and I

2nd Person *Oukou* - You (more than two)
3rd Person *Lakou* - They (more than two)
3rd Person *Lakou ala* - They (more than two over there)
3rd Person *Lakou nei* - They (more than two over here)

The first person plural also has two forms.

The first form is *kakou,* which signifies we, more than two, including the speaker and the person addressed.

E hele aku ana kakou signifies we will go (any number over two)

- I and the person or persons addressed.

The second form is *makou,* we (more than two) the speaker and his party, but excluding the person or persons addressed.

Ke hele nei makou signifies we go (any number over two) - I and those with me go, but not the person or persons addressed.

It must always be remembered, therefore, that the dual, *kaua,* and the plural, *kakou,* both include those addressed; while the dual, *maua,* and the plural, *makou,* do not include those addressed.

The irregularity of the two first persons, *kaua* and *maua* in the dual, and *kakou* and *makou* in the plural, may make it difficult to distinguish at first, but the problem will soon be overcome by repeated usage.

The "O Emphatic"

The "o emphatic" is an article used to point out the subject emphatically. It is used only in the nominative case and chiefly before pronouns and names of persons. It always appears before the name of a person in the nominative case.

There is no part of speech corresponding to it in the English language and, therefore, has no word into which it can be translated.

It is, however, of great use in the Hawaiian language for emphasis and euphony.

Exercise

Read and translate into English

Au, oe, oia, oiala, oinei, kaua, maua, olua, laua, laua ala, laua nei, kakou, makou, oukou, lakou, lakou ala, lakou nei, au, kaua, maua, kakou, makou, oe, olua, oukou, oia, laua, lakou, oiala, laua ala, lakou ala, oinei, laua nei, lakou nei, oinei, oiala, oia, oe, au, laua nei, laua ala, laua, olua, laua, kaua, lakou nei, lakou ala, lakou, oukou, makou, kakou, lakou nei, laua nei, oinei, lakou ala, laua ala, oiala, lakou, laua, oia, oukou, olua, oe, makou, maua, kakou, kaua, au.

Translate into Hawaiian

I, you, he, she, he (over there), she (over here), we (you and I), we (he and I), we (she and I), you (two), they (two), they (two over there), they (two over here), we (you, they and I), we (you, she and I), we (you, he and I), we (they and I), you (three), they (three), they (four, over there), they (three over here), he, she, he and she, they (two over there), they (three over here), he, she, he and she, they (two over here), she and he (over here), he (over here), she (over here), he (over there), they (three).

HAAWINA EKOLU
(Lesson Three)

Hola ehia keia? - What time is it?
Hola eiwa keia. - It is nine o'clock.

THE DEFINITE ARTICLE

The definite article is used as in English. However, there are three definite articles corresponding to the English "the." They are *ka* or *ke* for the singular and *na* for the plural.

Ka is used before all words beginning with *e, i, u, h, l, m, n* and *w* and some words beginning with *a, o* and *p*.

Ke is used before all words beginning with *k* and some words beginning with *a, o* and *p*.

The proper use of these articles can be learned through constant usage.

Vocabulary

a - and

ame - and

hoaaloha - friend
　ka hoaaloha - the friend
　na hoaaloha - friends; the friends

ka - the

kaikaina - younger brother of a boy; younger sister of a girl
　ke kaikaina - the younger brother of a boy; the younger sister of a girl

na kaikaina - younger brothers of a boy or of boys: younger sisters of a girl or of girls; the younger brothers of boys; the younger sisters of girls

kaikamahine - daughter; girl
　ke kaikamahine - the daughter; the girl
　na kaikamahine - daughters; the daughters; girls; the girls

kaikuaana - older brother of a boy; older sister of a girl

ke kaikuaana - the older brother of a boy; the older sister of a girl

na kaikuaana - older brothers of a boy or of boys; the older brothers of a boy or of boys; older sisters of a girl or of girls; the older sisters of a girl or of girls

kaikuahine - sister of a boy

ke kaikuahine - the sister of a boy

na kaikuahine - sisters of a boy or of boys; the sisters of a boy or of boys

kaikunane - brother of a girl

ke kaikunane - the brother of a girl

na kaikunane - brothers of a girl or of girls; the brothers of a girl or of girls

kanaka - man

ke kanaka - the man

na kanaka - men; the men

kane - husband, male person

ke kane - the husband; the male person

na kane - husbands; the husbands; male persons; the male persons

ke - the

keiki - child, boy, son

ke keiki - the boy, the child; the son

na keiki - boys; children; sons; the boys; the children; the sons

keiki kane - boy; male child; son

ke keiki kane - the boy; the male child; the son

na keiki kane - boys; the boys; male children; the male children; sons; the sons

kupuna - grand parent

ke kupuna - the grand parent

na kupuna - grandparents; the grandparents

kupuna kane - grandfather; granduncle

ke kupuna kane - the grandfather; the granduncle

na kupuna kane - grandfathers; granduncles; the grandfathers; the granduncles

kupuna wahine - grandmother; grandaunt

ke kupuna wahine - the grandmother; the grandaunt

na kupuna wahine - grandmothers; grandaunts; the grandmothers; the grandaunts

makua - parent

ka makua - the parent

na makua - parents; the parents

makuahine - mother; aunt

ka makuahine - the mother; the aunt

na makuahine - mothers; aunts; the mothers; the aunts

makuakane - father; uncle

ka makuakane - the father; the uncle

na makuakane - fathers; uncles; the fathers; the uncles

moopuna - grandchild

ka moopuna - the grandchild

na moopuna - the grandchildren

wahine - wife; woman

ka wahine - the wife; the woman

na wahine - women; the women; wives; the wives

Note: Unlike English, the definite article in Hawaiian has a plural number, thus we say *na* for the plural.

Read and translate into English

1. Ka makuakane, ka makuahine. 2. Ka makuahine ame ke keiki. 3. Ke keiki kane ame ke kaikamahine. 4. Ke kaikunane, na kaikuahine. 5. Ke kane ame ka wahine. 6. Na kaikunane ame na hoaaloha. 7. Ke kaikuahine ame ka hoaaloha. 8. Ka wahine ame ke keiki. 9. Ka makuakane, ka makuahine ame na keiki. 10. Ke kanaka, ke keikikane ame ke kaikamahine.

Translate into Hawaiian

1. The mother, the daughter. 2. The father and the sons. 3. The son and the mother. 4. The father and the mother. 5. The brother, the friend, the sister and the children. 6. The husband, the wife and the child. 7. The sister and the friends. 8. The daughter and the sons. 9. The man and the son. 10. The woman and the child. 11. The older sister and the younger sister. 12. The younger brother and the older brother.

Note: The articles, *ka, ke* or *na* must be repeated before each noun to designate singular or plural number.
Example: *Ke kaikamahine, ka makuahine ame na kupuna* - The daughter, mother and grandparents.

REVIEW

1. Lakou ala ame laua nei. 2. Ke kaikamahine, na hoaloha ame na keikikane. 3. Ke keikikane ame na makua. 4. Olua ame laua ala. 5. Na kane, na wahine ame na keiki. 6. Na keikikane, na makua ame na kupuna. 7. Maua, oukou ame lakou ala. 8. Na kane, na wahine ame na keiki. 9. Makou, oukou ame lakou nei. 10. Ke kupunakane, ke kupunawahine ame na moopuna.

1. The boys, the girls and the parents. 2. They (more than two, over here) and you (more than two). 3. The grandfathers, the grandmothers and the grandchildren. 4. You (two), they (two over here) and we (more than two). 5. You, they and I, and they (two). 6. They (more than two, over here) and you, they and I. 7. The women and children. 8. The men, women and children. 9. You (two) and they (two). 10. They (two over there) and they (more than two over here).

HAAWINA EHA
(Lesson Four)

Pehea oe? - How are you?
Maikai no. A pehea oe? - I am well. And how are you?
Maikai no au. I am well.

THE INDEFINITE ARTICLE

He is the Hawaiian indefinite article corresponding to the English "a" or "an." It is used only in the singular number and in the nominative case.

Mau or *po'e* follows *he* to form the dual or plural.
Example:

> *he hoaaloha* - a friend

> *he mau hoaaloha*
> *he po'e hoaaloha* - friends, some friends

NOTE: The term po'e is used only in relation to people.

I also expresses the indefinite article "a" or "an" and *i mau* expresses "some."
Example:

E lawe aku ana ke keiki kane i manako nau.
The boy will take a mango for you.

Ua lawe mai nei ke kaikamahine i apala na kaua.
The girl brought an apple for us (you and me).

E Mele e haawi mai oe i mau puke na maua.
Mary, give us (he and I or she and I) some books.

He is also used to make a statement as:

He hele au i ke kula - I go to school.
He hele ko'u kaikunane i ka hana - My brother goes to work.

Vocabulary

iole - mouse; rat
  he iole - a mouse; a rat
  he mau iole - mice, some mice, rats; some rats

ilio - dog
  he ilio - a dog
  he mau ilio - dogs, some dogs
hana - to work
  i ka hana - (goes) to work
  he hana oia - he works, she works
he - a declarative word
he - a, an
  he mau - plural sign; some
  he po'e - plural sign; some
hoaaloha - friend
  he hoaaloha - a friend
  he mau hoaaloha - friends; some friends
  he po'e hoaaloha - friends; some friends

kaa - car; carriage
  he kaa - a car; a carriage
  he mau kaa - cars; carriages; some cars; some carriages
kaikaina - younger brother of a boy; younger sister of a girl
  he kaikaina - a younger brother of a boy; a younger sister of a girl
  he mau kaikaina / he po'e kaikaina - younger brothers of a boy or of some boys; younger sisters of a girl or of some girls

kaikamahine - daughter; girl
  he kaikamahine - a daughter; a girl
  he mau kaikamahine / he po'e kaikamahine - daughters; girls; some daughters; some girls
kaikuaana - older brother of a boy; older sister of a girl
  he kaikuaana - an older brother of a boy; an older sister of a girl
  he mau kaikuaana / he po'e kaikuana - older brothers of a boy or of some boys; older sisters of a girl or of some girls
kaikuahine - sister of a boy
  he kaikuahine - a sister of a boy
  he mau kaikuahine / he po'e kaikuahine - sisters of a boy or of some boys
kaikunane - brother of a girl
  he kaikunane - a brother of a girl
  he mau kaikunane / he po'e kaikunane - brothers of a girl or of some girls

kauhale - home; house
  i kauhale - at home
kamalii - a plural word meaning children
kanaka - man
  he kanaka - a man
  he mau kanaka / he po'e kanaka - men; some men

kane - husband, male person

he kane - a husband; a male person

he mau kane / he po'e kane - husbands; some husbands; male persons; some male persons

keiki - boy, child, son

he keiki - a boy; a child; a son

he mau keiki / he po'e keiki - boys; some boys; children; some children; sons; some sons

keiki kane - boy; male child; son

he mau keiki kane / he po'e keiki kane - boys; some boys; children; some children; sons; some sons

kula - school

he kula - a school

he mau kula - schools; some schools

i ke kula - to school

kupuna - grand parent; forefather

he kupuna - a grandparent

he mau kupuna / he po'e kupuna - grandparents; some grandparents

kupuna kane - grandfather; granduncle

he kupuna kane - a grandfather; a granduncle

he mau kupuna kane / he po'e kupuna kane - grandfathers; some grandfathers; granduncles; some granduncles

kupuna wahine - grandmother; grandaunt

he kupuna wahine - a grandmother; a grandaunt

he mau kupuna wahine / he po'e kupuna wahine - grandmothers; grandaunts; some grandmothers; some grandaunts

lio - horse

he lio - a horse

he mau lio - horses, some horses

makua - parent

he makua - a parent

he mau makua / he po'e makua - parents; some parents

makuahine - mother; aunt

he makuahine - a mother; an aunt

he mau makuahine / he po'e makuahine - mothers, aunts, some mothers, some aunts

makuakane - father; uncle

he makuakane - a father; an uncle

he mau makuakane / he po'e makuakane - fathers; uncles; some fathers; some uncles

manako - mango

he manako - a mango

he mau manako - mangoes; some mangoes

noho - chair; saddle

i noho - a chair; a saddle

i noho nau? - a chair for you? a saddle for you?

i mau noho - some chairs; some saddles

he noho - a chair; a saddle

he mau noho - chairs; some chairs; saddles; some saddles

noholio - saddle

popoki - cat
  he popoki - a cat
  he mau popoki - cats; some
  cats

puke - book
  i puke - a book
  i puke nau? - a book for you?
  he puke - a book
  he mau puke - books; some
  books

Exercise

Read and translate into English

1. He makuakane a he makuahine. 2. He makuahine a he keiki. 3. He keiki a he kaikamahine. 4. He wahine, he kanaka a he mau keiki. 5. He kaikunane a he kaikuahine. 6. He kaikuaana a he kaikaina. 7. He poʻe kanaka a he poʻe kamalii. 8. He kaikunane, he kaikuahine a he mau hoaaloha. 9. He wahine a he mau keiki. 10. He mau kanaka, he mau keiki a he mau ilio. 11. He hele laua i ka auau kai. 12. He noho koʻu kaikuahine i kauhale. 13. He holo moku lakou. 14. He hana oia.

Translate into Hawaiian

1. A mother and a daughter. 2. A father and a son. 3. A son and a mother. 4. A father, a mother and some children. 5. A woman and children. 6. Some women and children. 7. A man, a woman and children. 8. A dog and a cat. 9. A cat and some mice. 10. A carriage and some horses. 11. He stays at home. 12. They (two) go swimming. 13. They (more than two) go sailing. 14. She works.

Note: The indefinite articles *he, he mau* or *he poʻe* must be repeated before each noun to designate singular or plural number.

HAAWINA ELIMA
(Lesson Five)

E hele ana oe ihea? Where are you going?
E hele ana au i ka hale kuai. I am going to the store.

THE DEMONSTRATIVE ADJECTIVES

The demonstrative adjective point out a particular object.
Keia expresses this; as, *keia papale* - this hat.

kela or *kena* expresses that. *Kena,* however, is used only to point out a specific object either in the possession of or near the person spoken to; as, *Kela kaikamahine me kela mau wahine* - that girl and those women. *Kena kaikamahine me oe* - that girl with you.

Plural number is designated by *mau* or *po'e* following the demonstratives; as, *keia mau hale* - these houses; *kela po'e wahine* - those women, *kena po'e keiki me oe* - those children with you.

Ala and *nei* are also used with the demonstratives. *Ala* can only be used with "that" and *nei* only with "this."

Examples:
E noho mai oe ma keia noho nei - You sit in this chair, here.
E noho aku ana au ma kela noho ala - I will sit in that chair, there.

Demonstrative adjectives, in Hawaiian, must be repeated before each noun which they modify: *E hanai mai oe i keia keiki ame keia kaikamahine* - Feed this boy and girl.

Vocabulary

i - to
ike - to see, to know
haawi - to give
  e haawi aku - give (away from me)
  e haawi mai - give (toward me)
haawina - lesson
  ka haawina - the lesson
  na haawina - lessons, the lessons
hanai - to feed
  e hanai aku - feed (them, there)
  e hanai mai - feed (them, here)
  e hanai iho - feed (them by you)
ho'iho'i - to return
  e ho'iho'i aku - take back; return that way
  e ho'iho'i mai - bring back; return this way
holoholona - animal
  he holoholona - an animal

he mau holoholona - animals; some animals
ka holoholona - the animal
na holoholona - animals; the animals
keia - this
  keia mau - these
  keia po'e - these; these people
kela - that
  kela mau - those
  kela po'e - those; those people
kena - that (near person addressed)
  kena mau - those (near persons addressed)
  kena po'e - those; those people (near person addressed)
lawe - to take
  lawe aku - take away (from person speaking)
  lawe mai - bring
noho - chair; saddle
noho - to sit, to live, to stay
  noho aku - sit there
  noho mai - sit here

Exercise

Read and translate into English

1. He noho keia po'e wahine i kauhale. 2. He hana kela po'e wahine. 3. E lawe aku oe i keia mau puke a e ho'iho'i mai i kena mau penikala. 4. Ke hoopaa nei keia po'e keiki i na haawina. 5. E lawe aku ana au i keia mau ilio. 6. Ke lawe mai nei kela po'e kanaka

i na lio. 7. Ua ho'iho'i mai nei lakou ala i kela mau noho. 8. E hanai iho oe i kena po'e keiki. 9. Ua hanai aku nei keia keiki i na holoholona. 10. E hele mai ana kela kaikamahine i ke kula.

Translate into Hawaiian

1. These men will take those horses. 2. We returned those chairs. 3. These women stay at home and those men go to work. 4. They (two) fed the animals. 5. Take these books and bring those pencils. 6. These boys studied the lessons. 7. Those girls will come to school. 8. These girls brought back these saddles and took those carriages. 9. These men took the horses. 10. The girls brought these dogs.

HAAWINA EONO
(Lesson Six)

Ihea aku nei oe? Where have you been?
I ke kauka aku nei au. I went to the doctor's.

DEMONSTRATIVE PRONOUNS

Demonstrative pronouns, like demonstrative adjectives, point out a particular object. However, they stand for the nouns; they do not modify them.

The demonstrative pronouns are *keia* (this); *kela* (that); *kena* (that); *keia mau* (these); *kela mau* (those); and *kena mau* (those).

Examples:
He noho paipai keia - This is a rocking chair.
He pakekau kela - That is a table.
He moena kena - That (near you) is a mat.
He mea kanu keia - This is a plant.
He mau kiele kena - Those (near you) are gardenias.
He mau ipukukui kela - Those are lamps.

Vocabulary

kukui - light
  ke kukui - the light
  na kukui - lights; the lights

ipukukui - lamp
  ka ipu kukui - the lamp
  na ipu kukui - lamps; the lamps
kukulu - to build, as a house
kula - school; gold
  ke kula - the school; the gold
  na kula - schools; the schools
  i ke kula - to school

hale kula - school, school building; school house
  ka hale kula - the school; the school building; the school house
  na hale kula - schools, school buildings; the schools, the school buildings

la pule - Sunday (lit. prayer day)
  i ka la pule - on Sunday
  i ka la pule nei - Sunday, just past
  i keia la pule a'e - next Sunday
  i kela la pule aku nei - last Sunday

maia - banana
  ka maia - the banana
  na maia - bananas, the bananas
Makaleka - Margaret
Maliana - Marian; Maryann
mea kanu - plant
Mele - Mary
mele - song
  Ka mele - the song
  na mele - songs; the songs

pakeke - bucket, pocket
  ka pakeke - the bucket, the pocket
  na pakeke - buckets, the buckets; pockets, the pockets
pio - to go out, as a fire or light
  ua pio - went out as a fire or light

pua - flower
  ka pua - the flower
  na pua - flowers; the flowers

Exercise

Read and translate into English

1. He hele keia po'e keiki i ka pule i ka la Pule. 2. La Pule keia. 3. He manako kela. 4. He kumukula kela a he haumana keia.

5. He hale pule kela. 6. He hale kula keia. 7. He popoki keia a he iole kela. 8. He keiki kane keia. 9. He kaa kela. 10. He pua keia a he mea kanu kela.

Translate into Hawaiian

1. That is a school. 2. Those people go to church on Sundays. 3. This is a church. 4. This is Sunday. 5. That is a cat and this is a dog. 6. This is a mango. 7. That is a teacher and this is a pupil. 8. Today is Sunday. 9. This is a plant. 10. That is a flower. 11. That (in your hand) is a lamp.

HAAWINA EHIKU
(Lesson Seven)

Hele aku nei oe ihea? Where did you go?
Hele aku nei au i ka halawai. I went to the meeting.

THE INDEFINITE ARTICLE AND THE VERB TO BE

There are no verbs in the Hawaiian language to express the idea of existence or being, like the verb "to be."

He combined with a personal pronoun in the nominative case, becomes the verb "to be" and expresses "am a, am an, is a, is an, are, are a" and "are an."

Examples:

He wahine Amelika au - I am an American woman.
He kanaka hana oe - you are a working man.
He kanaka kalaiwa kaa oia - he is a chauffeur.
He elemakule oiala - he (over there) is an old man.
He poʻe Kepani makou - we are Japanese people.
He wahine holoi lole oe - you are a washer woman.
He keiki Pelekane kela - that is an English boy.
He kaikamahine Pelekane oe - you are an English girl.
He kumukula au - I am a teacher.

Singular

He Amelika au - I am an American.
He Amelika oe - You are an American.
He Amelika oia - He is an American. She is an American.

He Amelika oiala - He (over there) is an American. She (over there) is an American.

He Amelika oinei - He (over here) is an American. She (over here) is an American.

Dual (two)

He mau Amelika kaua - We (you and I) are Americans.

He mau Amelika maua - We (he and I) are Americans; we (she and I) are Americans.

He mau Amelika olua - You (two) are Americans.

He mau Amelika laua - They (two) are Americans.

He mau Amelika laua ala - They (two over there) are Americans.

He mau Amelika laua nei - They (two over here) are Americans.

Plural (More than two)

He mau Amelika Kakou / He po'e Amelika kakou — We (you, they and I) are Americans; we (you, they and I) are American people.

He mau Amelika makou / He po'e Amelika makou — We (they and I) are Americans; we (they and I) are American people.

He mau Amelika oukou / He po'e Amelika oukou — You (more than two) are Americans; you (more than two) are American people.

He mau Amelika lakou / He po'e Amelika lakou — They (more than two) are Americans; they (more than two) are American people.

He mau Amelika lakou ala / He po'e Amelika lakou ala — They (more than two, over there) are Americans; they (more than two, over there) are American people.

He mau Amelika lakou nei / He po'e Amelika lakou nei — They (more than two, over here) are Americans; they (more than two, over here) are American people.

He mau Amelika na kaikamahine / He po'e Amelike na kaikamahine — The girls are Americans.

He mau Amelika keia mau kaikamahine / He po'e Amelika keia mau kaikamahine — These girls are Americans.

He mau Amelika kela mau kaikamahine / He po'e Amelika kela mau kaikamahine — Those girls are Americans.

Note: *Mau* denotes a smaller group of persons or things. *Poʻe* may be used in place of *mau* only in the plural number because it denotes a larger number of persons or things.

Exercise

Read and translate into English

1. He mau Pelekane maua. 2. He kumukula keia. 3. He mau kumukula laua nei. 4. He poʻe Kepani lakou ala. 5. He poʻe malihini lakou nei. 6. He mau keiki Amelika maua. 7. He mau haumana kaua. 8. He Palani maua. 9. He poʻe haumana oukou. 10. He kumukula oinei a he mau haumana laua ala.

Translate into Hawaiian

1. I am an American. 2. These are English children. 3. They, (over there) are Japanese. 4. They (over here) are Germans. 5. We (they and I) are teachers. 6. We (more than two) are strangers. 7. We (he and I) are visitors. 8. We (you, they and I) are French. 9. You are a stranger. 10. He is an Englishman.

HAAWINA EWALU
(Lesson Eight)

Aloha, ea! Greetings!
Ae, Aloha. Yes, greetings.
He malihini anei oe? Are you a stranger?
Ae, he malihini au. Yes, I am a stranger.

INTERROGATIVE OF THE VERB TO BE

In the interrogative sentences "am I?" "Are you?" "Is he?" etc., the word *anei* must follow the subject. However, when an adjective follows the subject, *anei* follows the adjective.

Examples:
Singular
He keiki kamaina anei au? - Am I a native born boy?
He kaikamahine hana anei oe? - Are you a working girl?
He wahine Haole anei oia? - Is she a white (caucasian) woman?
He kanaka Kepani anei oiala? - Is he (over there) a Japanese man?
He keiki Pake anei oinei? - Is he (over here) a Chinese boy?

Dual (Two)

He mau malihini anei kaua? - Are we (you and I) strangers?

He mau kamaaina anei maua? - Are we (he and I / she and I) residents?

He mau kaikamahine hana anei olua? - Are you (two) working girls?

He mau wahine Haole anei laua? - Are they (two) white women?

He mau keiki Kepani anei laua ala? - Are they (two over there) Japanese boys?

He mau kumukula anei laua nei? - Are they (two over here) school teachers?

Plural (More than two)

He poʻe haumana anei kakou? - Are we (you, they and I) students?

He poʻe kumukula anei makou? - Are we (they and I) school teachers?

He poʻe malihini anei oukou? - Are you (more than two) strangers?

He poʻe kamaaina anei lakou? - Are they (more than two) old timers?

He poʻe Kelemania anei lakou ala? - Are they (more than two over there) Germans?

He poʻe Lukini anei lakou nei? - Are they (more than two over here) Russians?

Vocabulary

anei - an interrogative word, "is he," "is she," "are they," "am I," "are you"

ilihune - poor

opiopio - young

Haole - a white person

himeni - to sing

kamaaina - native born; resi-dent; villager; old timer

kolohe - naughty; bad; dishonest

Lukini - Russian

maikaʻi - good

malihini - stranger; newcomer, guest

Pake - Chinese

waiwai - rich; property; estate

Exercise

Read and translate into English

1. He opiopio anei keia kanaka? 2. He luahine anei oinei? 3. He ilihune anei keia po'e kanaka? 4. He waiwai anei kela wahine? 5. He malihini anei oukou? 6. He kanaka hana anei kela? 7. He po'e wahine waiwai anei lakou ala? 8. He himeni anei kela kaikamahine? 9. He keiki kolohe anei keia? 10. He mau kumukula anei keia mau wahine?

Translate into Hawaiian

1. Is that a working man? 2. Is that man rich? 3. Do those girls sing? 4. Is she (over here) a working woman? 5. Are those men strangers? 6. Are these boys old timers? 7. Is this girl a stranger? 8. Does this girl work? 9. Does that boy go to school? 10. Is that a working man? 11. Is he a student? 12. Are those men school teachers?

HAAWINA HELUHELU

Auwe! - Oh!
e hele me oe - to go with you
e hele ana - walking, going
e hele nei - walking, going
e hele ana oe ihea? - where are you going?
e hele like kaua - let us go together
hele mai - come
i maila ke keiki kane - the boy said
halawai laua - they met
ku laua a walaau - they stood and talked
ma ke alanui - on the road
makemake au - I want
pane mai - answered

He kaikamahine kela e hele ana ma ke alanui a he keiki kane keia e hele nei ma ke alanui. Halawai laua. Ku laua a walaau.

I maila ke keiki kane. "E hele ana oe ihea?"

"E hele ana au i kahakai." Pane mai ke kaikamahine.

"Auwe! makemake au e hele me oe."

"Hele mai. E hele like kaua i kahakai."

A store and hotel in Kaunakakai.

HAAWINA EIWA
(Lesson Nine)

Mai hea mai nei oe? Where did you come from?
Mai Maui mai nei au. I came from Maui.

THE NEGATIVE AOLE

To form the negative with the verb "to be," the sentence begins with the word *aole* (not) and the pronoun or noun precedes the indefinite article.

Examples:
Singular
Aole au he kaikamahine hana - I am not a working girl.
Aole oe he keiki kamaaina - you are not a native boy.
Aole oia he wahine haole - she is not a white woman.
Aole oiala he kanaka Kepani - he (over there) is not a Japanese man.
Aole oinei he keiki Pake - he (over here) is not a Chinese boy.
Aole ke keiki he Kelemania - the boy is not German.
Aole keia keiki he Palani - this boy is not French.
Aole kela keiki he Pelekane - that boy is not English.

Dual (Two)

Aole kaua he mau malihine - we (you and I) are not strangers.

Aole maua he mau kamaaina - we (he and I / she and I) are not residents.

Aole olua he mau kaikamahine hana - you (two) are not working girls.

Aole laua he mau wahine haole - they (two) are not white women.

Aole laua ala he mau keiki Kepani - they (two over there) are not Japanese boys.

Aole laua nei he mau kumukula - they (two over here) are not teachers.

Aole na keiki he mau haumana - the boys are not students.

Aole keia mau keiki he mau kanaka hana - these boys are not working men.

Aole kela mau keiki he mau kalaiwa kaa - those boys are not chauffers.

Plural (more than two)

Aole kakou he po'e haumana - we (you, they and I) are not students.

Aole makou he po'e kumukula - we (they and I) are not teachers.

Aole oukou he po'e malihini - you (more than two) are not strangers.

Aole lakou he po'e kamaaina - they (more than two) are not old timers.

Aole lakou ala he po'e Kelemania - they (more than two over there) are not Germans.

Aole lakou nei he po'e Lukini - they (more than two over here) are not Russians.

Aole na keiki he po'e malihini - the boys are not strangers.

Aole keia po'e keiki he po'e mahiai - these boys are not farmers.

Aole kela po'e keiki he po'e Amelika - those boys are not Americans.

Exercise

Read and translate into English

1. Aole oia he kumukula. 2. Aole oe he Palani. 3. Aole au he

Kelemania.   4. Aole oia he Hawaii.   5. Aole laua nei he mau elemakule. 6. Aole laua he mau Kepani. 7. Aole oinei he Lukini. 8. Aole makou he po'e Pelekane. 9. Aole kakou he po'e haumana. 10. Aole laua ala he mau keiki Hawaii.

Translate into Hawaiian

1. I am not a German. 2. He is not an old man. 3. We (you and I) are not strangers. 4. We (he and I) are not students. 5. He (over there) is not Hawaiian. 6. You (two) are not Germans. 7. That is not candy. 8. We (they and I) are not French. 9. You (more than two) are not Americans. 10. You are not an Englishman.

HAAWINA UMI
(Lesson Ten)

PERSONAL PRONOUNS
Possessive Case (First Group)

In Hawaiian, as in English, personal pronouns change in form to indicate case.

Possessive pronouns indicate possession. The possessive pronoun in Hawaiian is governed by the thing possessed and not, as in English, by the possessor.

There are two forms of the possessive pronouns, the *o* and the *a;* as *ko'u papale* (my hat), *ka'u popoki* (my cat). They are simply the personal pronouns in the nominative case (Haawina Elua) preceded by the prepositions *a* or *o, ka* or *ko* and *na* or *no,* thus dividing them into three groups. There is no difference in the meaning of these forms; the difference lies in their use.

There is an important distinction between the three *a* groups of prepostions *a, ka* and *na* and the three *o* groups of prepositions *o, ko* and *no.*

The *o* form of the possessive, *o, ko* or *no,* governs what the possessor uses, wears or is otherwise affected by and any occurances over which he has no control such as his birth or his given name.

It has to do with God and his universe; the possessor's country, his estate, land, home, etc.

In human relationships, it governs his ancestors, parents,

brothers, sisters, friends, supervisors, rulers, employers, land-lords, teachers, superiors and people of the earth.

It governs natural or inherited qualities or faculties of the mind such as thought, knowledge, intellect, memories, emotions, senses such as hearing, seeing, feeling, etc.

It also governs the human body and all its parts, life, illness, pain, death, etc.; his arrivals and departures, all which protects the body, as any shelter, home and its furniture, his clothes or any object of adornment; whatever transports the body such as horses, airplanes, ships, automobiles, etc.; all that represents his body such as portraits, etc.

The *a* form of the possessive, *a, ka* or *na* governs what the possessor produces or controls.

In human relationships, it governs husbands, wives, children, descendants, dependants or subordinates such as one's employees, pupils, servants, etc.

It also governs one's compositions such as music; anything he may write, as his story, letter, lesson, etc. or any oral expressions, as his speech.

It controls one's craft and the implements he uses such as tools, utensils, equipment, etc.

Also small objects as cameras, toys, books, dishes, one's personal toilet articles, etc.

All animals except those used to transport a human being.

However, we have the possessive pronouns *kuu* (my), which is used for either *kaʻu* or *koʻu* and *ko* (your), which is used for either *kau* or *kou.* These pronouns, *kuu* and *ko,* are more familiar, and can be used in place of the regular forms, *kaʻu, koʻu, kau* or *kou,* without being at a loss as to which is the proper word to use.

Examples:
Singular
kaʻu, koʻu, kuu - my
kau, ko, kou - your
kana, kona - his, her
ka iala, ko iala - his, her (over there)
ka ianei, ko ianei - his, her (over here)

Dual (Two)

ka kaua, ko kaua - our, (your and my)
ka maua, ko maua - our (his and my / her and my)
ka olua, ko olua - your, (two)
ka laua, ko laua - their (two)
ka laua ala, ko laua ala - their (two over there)
ka laua nei, ko laua nei - their (two over here)

Plural (More than two)

ka kakou, ko kakou - our (your, her and my / your, his and my / your, their and my)
ka makou, ko makou - our (his, her and my / their and my)
ka oukou, ko oukou - your (more than two)
ka lakou, ko lakou - their (more than two)
ka lakou ala, ko lakou ala - their (more than two over there)
ka lakou nei, ko lakou nei - their (more than two over here)

Ka* Keoni peni keia - This is John's pen.
Ko* Makaleka papale kela - That is Margaret's hat.
Haawi mai oe i ka Keoni peni - Give me John's pen.
E hoʻihoʻi aku oe i ko Makaleka papale - Take back Margaret's hat.
Ka Pekelo puke keia - This is Peter's book.
Ko Malia kuka kela - That is Mary's coat.
E kahea aku oe i kou kaikunane, ia Hale - Call your brother, Harry.
E kahea mai oe i kou kaikuahine, ia Mele - Call your sister, Mary.
E Mele, e hanai iho oe i kou kaikaina - Mary, feed your younger sister.
Ka Mele keiki - Mary's son; Mary's child
Ka Keoni mau keiki - John's children
Ko Iokepa makuahine - Joseph's mother
Ke hele mai nei ko Makaleka mau kaikaina - Margaret's younger sisters are coming.
Ua hoʻi aku nei ko Aukake mau kaikuahine - August's sisters went home.
Ua hoʻi mai nei ko Ane kaikunane - Annie's brother came back.
Ua komo mai nei o Elikapeka i kona kuka - Elizabeth wore her coat.
E haawi aku oe ia Lopaka i kana penikala - Give Robert his pen.

---

*Ka or *ko* before names of persons signifies the apostrophe "s."

Exercise

Read and translate into English

1. Ua ho‘i mai nei ka‘u keiki e ike ia‘u. 2. E hele aku ana makou i ka home o ko‘u mau makua. 3. Makemake au e ike i kuu makuahine ame kuu mau keiki. 4. O kau keiki anei keia? 5. Aole anei kela ke kaikamahine o kou kaikuahine? 6. Ke lawe mai nei ko‘u kaikunane i kana mau keiki. 7. E himeni mai oe i na mele o ke kula. 8. Ua haawi aku nei o Mele i ka aina i kana mau keiki. 9. He kumukula anei oe? 10. Aole, aole au he kumukula, he wahine hana au.

Translate into Hawaiian

1. My brother brings his children. 2. My son came home to see me. 3. Sing the songs of the school. 4. We will go to the home of my parents. 5. Mary gave the land to her children. 6. I wish to see my mother and my children. 7. Are you a teacher? 8. No, I am not a teacher, I am a working woman. 9. Is this your son? 10. No, he is the son of my brother.

HAAWINA UMIKUMAMAKAHI
(Lesson Eleven)

E hele ana oe i ka halawai?
Ae, e hele ana au i ka halawai.

THE INDEFINITE ARTICLE AND THE VERB "TO HAVE"

The indefinite article "he" (Lesson Three) includes the verb "to have," when it is used with the first group of possessive pronouns (Lesson Ten).

Examples:
Singular
He apala ka'u - I have an apple.
He alani kau - You have an orange.
He manako kana - He has a mango. / She has a mango.
He kuawa kaiala - He/She (over there) has a guava.
He ohelo kainei - He/She (over here) has a strawberry.
He apala ka ke kaikamahine - The girl has an apple.
He alani ka keia keiki - This boy has an orange.
He manako ka kela wahine - That woman has a mango.

Dual (Two)

He mau apala ka kaua - We (you and I) have apples / We (you and I) have some apples.

He mau alani ka maua - We (he/she and I) have oranges; we (he/she and I) have some oranges.

He mau manako ka olua - You (two) have mangoes; you (two) have some mangoes.

He mau kuawa ka laua - They (two) have guavas; they (two) have some guavas.

He mau ohelo ka laua ala - They (two over there) have strawberries / some strawberries.

He mau apala ka laua nei - They (two over here) have apples / some apples.

He mau apala ka na keiki - The boys have apples / some apples.

He mau alani ka keia mau kaikamahine - These girls have oranges / some oranges.

He mau manako ka kela mau kanaka - Those men have mangoes / some mangoes.

Plural (More than two)

He mau apala ka kakou - We (you, he/she and I) have apples / we (you, they and I) have some apples.

He mau alani ka makou - We (he, she and I) have oranges; we (they and I) have some oranges.

He mau manako ka oukou - You (more than two) have mangoes / some mangoes.

He mau kuawa ka lakou - They (more than two) have guavas / some guavas.

He mau ohelo ka lakou ala - They (more than two over there) have strawberries / some strawberries.

He mau apala ka lakou nei - They (more than two over here) have apples / some apples.

He mau alani ka na keiki - The boys have oranges / some oranges.

Vocabulary of Nouns

Ke ahi - the fire; the match.

Ka ipukukui - the lamp.

Ka hopuna olelo - the sentence.

Ke kukui - the light.

Ke kumu laau - the tree.

Ka lio - the horse.

Ka mele - the song.

Ka moolelo - the story.

Ka niho - the tooth.

Ka pepa - the paper.

Ka poohiwi - the shoulder.

Ka poli - the bosom.

Exercise

Read and translate into English

1. He mau popoki ka'u. 2. He mau ilio kana. 3. He penikala kau. 4. He peni ka Makaleka. 5. He alani ka iala. 6. He ipukukui ka Mele. 7. He puke ka ianei. 8. He lole kona. 9. He mau puke ka Keoni. 10. He mau papale ko Keaka. 11. He mau keiki ka laua. 12. He mau kupuna ko makou.

Translate into Hawaiian

1. These girls have oranges. 2. Those boys have apples. 3. Margaret has a horse. 4. He has a wife. 5. John has some books. 6. Jack has some hats. 7. They have children. 8. We have some coats. 9. I have some dresses. 10. I have a book. 11. Mary has an orange. 12. Margaret has a hat.

HAAWINA UMIKUMAMALUA
(Lesson Twelve)

Poʻahia keia? What day is this?
Poʻakahi keia. This is Monday.

THE INTERROGATIVE OF THE VERB "TO HAVE"

Anei is an interrogative word. It follows the noun in a sentence, as:

He penikala anei kaʻu? Have I a pencil? or Do I have a pencil?
He papale anei kou? Have you a hat? or Do you have a hat?

Examples:
Singular
He ilio anei kaʻu? - Do I have a dog? Have I a dog?
He popoki anei kau? - Do you have a cat? Have you a cat?
He kao anei kana? - Does he/she have a goat? Has he/she a goat?
He pipi anei ka iala? - Does he/she (over there) have a cow? Has he/she (over there) a cow?
He lapaki anei ka ianei? - Does he/she (over here) have a rabbit? Has he/she (over here) a rabbit?
He popoki anei ka ke kaikamahine? - Does the girl have a cat? Has the girl a cat?
He ilio anei ka keia keiki? - Does this boy have a dog? Has this boy a dog?
He pipi anei ka Mele? - Does Mary have a cow? Has Mary a cow?

Dual (Two)

He mau kao anei ka kaua? - Do we (you and I) have goats? Have we (you and I) any goats?

He mau haumana anei ka maua? - Do we (he/she and I) have pupils? Have we (he/she and I) any pupils?

He mau keiki anei ka olua? - Do you (two) have children? Have you (two) any children?

He pipi anei ka laua - Do they (two) have a cow? Have they (two) a cow?

He hipa anei ka laua ala? - Do they (two over there) have a sheep? Have they (two over there) a sheep?

He mau hipa anei ka laua nei? - Do they (two over here) have some sheep? Have they (two over here) some sheep?

He ilio anei ka keia mau keiki? - Do these children have a dog? Have these children a dog?

He hoki anei ka Manuela ma* - Do Manuel and another or others have a mule? Have Manuel and another or others a mule?

Plural (More than two)

He mau haumana anei ka kakou? - Do we (you, he/she/they and I) have pupils?

He kuene anei ka makou? - Do we (he, she and I) have a waiter? Have we (they and I) a waiter?

He mau kuene anei ka oukou? - Do you (more than two) have any waiters? Have you (more than two) any waiters?

He wahine hana anei ka lakou? - Do they (more than two) have a maid? Have they (more than two) a maid?

He kanaka hana anei ka lakou ala? - Do they (more than two over there) have a man servant? Have they (more than two over there) a man servant?

---

* *ma* after the name of a person signifies one or more persons than the one named.

He mau keiki anei ka lakou nei? - Do they (more than two over here) have any children? Have they (more than two over here) any children?

He mau keiki anei ka keia po'e wahine? - Do these women have any children? Have these women any children?

He mau keiki anei ka Keoki laua me Malia? - Do George and Mary have any children? Have George and Mary any children?

Singular

He palule anei ko'u? - Do I have a shirt? Have I a shirt?

He kuka anei kou? - Do you have a coat? Have you a coat?

He paa kamaa anei kona? - Does he/she have a pair of shoes? Has he/she a pair of shoes?

He papale anei ko iala? - Does he/she (over there) have a hat? Has he/she (over there) a hat?

He kuka anei ko ianei? - Does he/she (over here) have a coat? Has he/she (over here) a coat?

He lole anei ko Mele? - Does Mary have a dress? Has Mary a dress?

He palule anei ko Keoki? - Does George have a shirt? Has George a shirt?

Dual (Two)

He papale kapu anei ko kaua? - Do we (you and I) have a cap? Have we (you and I) a cap?

He palule anei ko maua? - Do we (he/she and I) have a shirt? Have we (he/she and I) a shirt?

He kuka anei ko olua? - Do you (two) have a coat? Have you (two) a coat?

He papale anei ko laua? - Do they (two) have a hat? Have they (two) a hat?

He lole anei ko laua ala? - Do they (two over there) have a dress? Have they (two over there) a dress?

He papale anei ko laua nei? - Do they (two over here) have a hat? Have they (two over here) a hat?

He kamaa anei ko keia mau keiki? - Do these boys have shoes? Do these children have shoes? Have these boys/children any shoes?

He mau kuka anei ko Maliana ma? - Do Maryann and another have coats? Have Maryann and the others any coats?

Plural (More than two)

He mau palule anei ko kakou? - Do we (you, he/she and I) have shirts? Have we (you, he/she and I) any shirts? Have we (you, they and I) any shirts?

He mau kuka anei ko makou? - Do we (he, she and I) have coats? Do we (they and I) have coats? Have we (they and I) any coats?

He mau makua anei ko oukou? - Do you (more than two) have parents? Have you (more than two) any parents?

He mau kupuna anei ko lakou? - Do they (more than two) have grandparents? Have they (more than two) grandparents?

He mau kumukula anei ko lakou ala? - Do they (more than two over there) have teachers? Have they (more than two over there) any teachers?

He mau kaikunane anei ko kela mau kaikamahine? - Do those girls have brothers? Have those girls any brothers?

He mau kaikuahine anei ko kela mau keiki kane? - Do those boys have sisters? Have those boys any sisters?

Note: The word *no* is used in place of *anei* to answer the foregoing questions, as: *Ae, he kaikuahine no ko kela mau keiki kane.*

The word *no* may be used in place of *anei* in asking a question.

Vocabulary

ae - yes

aohe - does not have; has not

aohe a'u - I do not have; I have no

aole - no

ike - to see; to know

inika - ink
  he inika - ink; some ink
  ka inika - ink; the ink

kaikamahine - girl; daughter
  he kaikamahine - a girl; a daughter
  ke kaikamahine - the girl; the daughter

kanaka - man
  he kanaka - a man
  ke kanaka - the man

keiki - boy; son
  he keiki - a boy; a son
  ke keiki - the boy; the son

naloale - to be lost

peni - pen
  he peni - a pen
  ka peni - the pen

penikala - pencil
  he penikala - a pencil
  ka penikala - the pencil

pepa - paper
  he pepa - paper; a paper
  ka pepa - the paper

puke - book
  he puke - a book
  ka puke - the book

puke a'o olelo - grammar
  he puke a'o olelo - a grammar
  ka puke a'o olelo - the grammar

wai - water
  he wai - some water
  ka wai - the water

wahine - wife; woman
  he wahine - a wife; a woman
  ka wahine - the wife; the woman

Exercise

Read and translate into English

1. He kaikunane no kou? 2. Ae, he kaikunane no ko'u. 3. He Kaikuahine no kona? 4. Aole, aohe ona kaikuahine. 5. He keiki no

kau? 6. Aole, aohe a'u keiki, he kaikamahine ka'u. 7. Ua ike anei oe i kana keiki? 8. Ae, ua ike au i kana keiki. 9. Ua ike anei oe i kona makuahine? 10. Ae, ua ike au i kona makuahine.

Translate into Hawaiian

1. Do you have a son? 2. No, I do not have a son. 3. Have you a daughter? 4. Yes, I have a daughter. 5. Does she have a brother? 6. No, she does not have a brother. 7. Do the girls have coats? 8. Yes, they have coats. 9. Have you a dress? 10. No, I do not have a dress. 11. Have those boys any sisters? 12. Yes, they have sisters. 13. Have these girls seen their mother? 14. Yes, they have seen their mother.

HAAWINA UMIKUMAMAKOLU
(Lesson Thirteen)

E hele kaua i ka halawai. Let us go to the meeting.
Oia, e hele kaua. All right, let us go. Fine let's go.

PERSONAL PRONOUNS
Possessive Case (Second Group)

The second group of possessive pronouns is a combination of the simple preposition *a* or *o* (of) and the personal pronouns in the nominative case (Lesson One).

The *a* of the pronoun *au*, first person singular, is dropped when used with either *a* or *o*; that is, instead of using *a au* or *o au*, the words become *a'u* or *o'u*.

The pronoun *oe*, second person singular (Lesson Two) is dropped and the words *au* or *ou* are used in its place; thus, instead of using *a oe* or *o oe*, the words become *au* or *ou*.

The words used for the first person *a'u*, *o'u* are pronounced with a break between the two vowels, while the words used for the second person *au*, *ou* are slurred together.

The pronoun *oia*, third person singular, is dropped and the word *na* is used in its place; thus, instead of *a oia* or *o oia*, the words become *ana* or *ona*. However, with the particles *ala* or *nei*, the pronoun *ia*, third person singular, is used, but the *a* is dropped and the letter *i* is joined to the particle for the sake of euphony, and the words become *aiala* and *ainei*.

Examples:

Singular

a'u; o'u - of me; my

au; ou - of you; your

ana; ona - of him; his; of her; her

aiala - of him (over there); his (over there); of her (over there); her (over there)

ainei - of him / of her (over here); his / her (over here)

Dual (Two)

a kaua; o kaua - of us (you and me); our (your and my)

a maua; o maua - of us (him/her and me); our (his/her and my)

a olua; o olua - of you (two); your (two)

a laua; o laua - of them (two); their (two)

a laua ala; o laua ala - of them (two over there); their (two over there)

a laua nei; o laua nei - of them (two over here); their (two over here)

Plural (more than two)

a kakou; o kakou - of us (you, them and me); our (your, their and my)

a makou; o makou - of us (them and me); our (their and my)

a oukou; o oukou - of you (more than two); your (more than two)

a lakou; o lakou - of them (more than two); their (more than two)

a lakou ala; o lakou ala - of them / their (more than two over there)

a lakou nei; o lakou nei - of them / their (more than two over here)

HAAWINA UMIKUMAMAHA
(Lesson Fourteen)

E aha ana oe? What are you doing?
E noho ana no. Just sitting.

THE NEGATIVE AOHE

To form the negative with the verb "to have" (Lesson Eleven) the sentence begins with the negative word *a'ohe* (have not) used with the second group of possessive pronouns.

Examples:
Singular

a'ohe a'u apala - I have no apple; I do not have an apple.

a'ohe au alani - you have no orange; you do not have an orange

a'ohe ana manako - he/she has no mango; he/she does not have a mango

a'ohe a iala kuawa - he/she (over there) has no guava; he/she (over there) does not have a guava.

a'ohe a ianei ohelo - he/she (over here) has no strawberry; he/she (over here) does not have a strawberry.

a'ohe a ke kaikamahine apala / a'ohe apala a ke kaikamahine - the girl has no apple; the girl does not have an apple.

a'ohe a keia keiki alani / a'ohe alani a keia keiki - This boy has no orange; this boy does not have an orange.

a'ohe manako a kela wahine - that woman has no mango; that woman does not have a mango.

Dual (Two)

a'ohe a kaua apala - we (you and I) have no apple; we (you and I) do not have an apple

a'ohe a maua alani - we (he/she and I) have no orange; we (he/she and I) do not have an orange.

a'ohe a olua manako - you (two) have no mango; you (two) do not have a mango.

a'ohe a laua kuawa - they (two) have no guava; they (two) do not have any guava.

a'ohe a laua ala kuawa - they (two over there) have no guava; they (two over there) do not have any guava.

a'ohe a laua nei ohelo - they (two over here) have no strawberries; they (two over here) do not have any strawberries.

a'ohe a na keiki apala - the boys/children have no apples; the boys/children do not have apples.

a'ohe alani a keia mau kaikamahine - these girls have no oranges; these girls do not have oranges.

a'ohe manako a kela mau kanaka - those men have no mangoes; those men do not have mangoes.

Plural (more than two)

a'ohe a kakou mau apala - we (you, he/she and I) have no apples; we (you, they and I) do not have apples.

a'ohe a makou alani - we (he, she and I) have no oranges; we (they and I) do not have oranges.

a'ohe a oukou manako - you (more than two) have no mangoes; you (more than two) do not have mangoes.

a'ohe a lakou kuawa - they (more than two) have no guavas; they (more than two) do not have guavas.

a'ohe a lakou ala ohelo - they (more than two over there) have no strawberries; they (more than two over there) do not have strawberries.

a'ohe a lakou nei apala - they (more than two over here) have no apples; they (more than two over here) do not have any apples.

a'ohe a na keiki alani - the boys/children have no oranges; the boys/children do not have any oranges.

HAAWINA UMIKUMAMALIMA
(Lesson Fifteen)

NOUNS

Nouns, as in English, are names of persons, places and things and are divided into two classes - proper and common.

Nouns are singular or plural unless otherwise designated.

They do not change in form to indicate whether singular, dual or plural in number.

The definite article *ka* or *ke* indicates singular nouns, and *na* the plural, as, *ka wahine* - the woman; *ke kanaka* - the man; *na keiki* - the children.

Other plural forms are *mau* and *po'e*, as *mau noho* - some chairs; *po'e kanaka* - some people.

Dual number is designated by *elua* (two) and *laua me* (he or she and another).

Example:

E hele aku ana no kanaka elua i ka lawaia - the two men will go fishing.

Ua hele mai nei o Mele laua me Pila e ike ia kaua - Mary and Bill came to see us.

Another plural form is the word *ma* following the name of a person, signifying the person named and one other or several others with him.

Example:

Ua hele mai nei o Iokepa ma - Joseph and another (or others) came.

Some nouns change the accent to form the plural.
Examples:

e-le-ma-kú-le - old man   *e-le-má-ku-le* - old men
ka-ná-ka - man   *ká-na-ka* - men
lu-a-hí-ne - old woman   *lu-á-hi-ne* - old women
wa-hí-ne - woman   *wá-hi-ne* - women

There are no words to express neuter gender or to give the idea of gender to any nouns that are neither male nor female.

There is nothing in Hawaiian to denote the gender of nouns, except the use of the adjective *kane* - male, and *wahine* - female; as *moa* - chicken; *moa wahine* - female chicken, hen; *moa kane* - male chicken, rooster.

There are also specific words that distinguish gender; as, old man - *elemakule;* old woman - *luahine;* female breeder - *kumulau.*

A noun or pronoun may be in the nominative case, the possessive case or the objective case.

Hawaiian nouns are not declined by any variations of their terminations as they are in English. The possessive case is formed by prefixing the words *ka* or *ko* or the simple prepositions *a* or *o*, *na* or *no.* The objective case is formed by prefixing the simple preposition *i* or *ia.*

Vocabulary of Nouns

Singular	Plural
ke ahi - the fire, the match	**na ahi** - the fires, the matches
ka ipuhao - the pot	**na ipuhao** - the pots
ka ipupaka - the (smoking) pipe	**na ipupaka** - the pipes
ka haawina - the lesson	**na haawina** - the lessons
ka hale - the house, the building	**na hale** - the houses, the buildings

ke kahi - the comb   na kahi - the combs
ke kumukula - the teacher   na kumukula - the teachers
ka mea ai - the food   na mea ai - the foods

ke paipu - the (water) pipe   na paipu - the pipes
ke pakaukau - the table   na pakaukau - the tables
ka penikala - the pencil   na penikala - the pencils
ka puke - the book   na puke - the books

Exercise

Read and translate into English

1. Ke kumukula, he mau haawina ame na puke. 2. Ka wahie, ke ahi a he ipuhao. 3. Ka hale, ka wahine, ke kane, ka ipupaka. 4. Ka home, ka makuakane, ka makuahine ame na keiki. 5. Ke pa, ka pakaukau ame ka mea ai. 6. Ke kaikamahine, ke keikikane ame na hoaaloha. 7. He mau kanaka, he mau noho ame na nupepa. 8. O olua, oiala ame laua nei. 9. Ka pahi, ke o ame na puna. 10. He papale, he lole a he mau kamaa.

Translate into Hawaiian

1. A boy, a girl and some friends. 2. A teacher, the lessons and some books. 3. The men, the chairs, and some newspapers. 4. The wood, a fire and some pots. 5. You and I, she (over here) and they (more than two over there). 6. A house, a man, a woman and a pipe. 7. A knife, a fork and some spoons. 8. The home, the father, mother and children. 9. A hat, a coat and some shoes. 10. Some plates, the table and food.

Review

au, kaua, maua, kakou, makou, oe, olua, oukou, oia, laua, lakou, oiala, laua ala, lakou ala, oinei, laua nei, lakou nei, lakou, lakou ala, lakou, oukou, makou, kakou, laua nei, laua ala, laua, olua, maua, kaua, oinei, oiala, oia, oe, au.

They (more than two over here); they (two over here); he (over here); she (over there); we (you and I); they (two); they (more than two); I; you; he; she; they (two); he (over there); I; we (you and I); we (he and I); you; he; you (more than two); we (you, they and I); we (they and I).

Old sugar mill in Kalae, Molokai.

HAAWINA UMIKUMAMAONO
(Lesson Sixteen)

VERBS

Verbs are words which indicate action, passion or a certain quality of their subjects.

Verbs have mood, tense, voice, number and person. Their functions and definitions are the same as in English.

The distinction of mood, tense and voice are expressed by separate little words. The number of a verb is not expressed by the verb itself, but by the noun or pronoun used.

The natural division of tenses are present, past and future. The verbal combination changes to form tenses, as will be seen in the conjugation of verbs.

Vocabulary of Verbs

ae - to agree, to consent, to permit

a'o - to teach

iho - to descend, to go down

ike - to see, to perceive

olelo - to say, to speak, to tell something to someone

hoopaa - to fasten, to study

hoopaa naau - to memorize

holo - to run, to sail in a boat

kuai - to buy, to sell

nana - to look, to look at

ninau - to ask a question

noi - to ask for something, to ask permission

pane - to answer

pii - to ascend, to climb

Exercise

Read and translate into English

1. E nana i na papale. 2. E a'o i na keiki. 3. E hoopaa i ka haawina. 4. He kaikunane ko'u. 5. E pane aku i ke kumukula. 6. E kuai i ke kuka. 7. E holo aku olua. 8. He luahine au. 9. E pii aku oukou iluna. 10. E nana mai i ka makuakane ame ka makuahine.

Translate into Hawaiian

1. Teach the children. 2. Look at the hat. 3. I have a sister. 4. Study the lessons. 5. Look at the father and the mother. 6. Answer the teacher. 7. Buy the hat. 8. You (two) run. 9. I am an old lady. 10. You climb.

HAAWINA UMIKUMAMAHIKU
(Lesson Seventeen)

VERBAL DIRECTIVES

Hawaiian verbs have motions in certain directions. These motions are expressed by *mai, aku, iho* and *aʻe,* which are called verbal directives; they follow the verb as closely as the construction of the sentence allows. Even those verbs expressing the most inactive state have these peculiarities.

Mai implies motion toward the speaker. It also denotes that the action is directed, not only toward the speaker, but toward someone or something near him.

Aku implies motion away from the speaker. It also denotes that the action is directed toward the person spoken to, and also toward someone or something near him or away from him, but further removed from the speaker.

Aʻe is used to express ascending motion or any motion sideways.

The word *pii* means to ascend. *Aku* or *mai* may be used with it instead of *aʻe.* When a person says, *"E pii aku oe,"* he means to go up away from him. On the other hand if he says *"E pii mai oe,"* he means to come up toward him.

Iho implies a downward motion.

Note: When speaking of oneself, the directive *iho* is used; as, myself - *iaʻu iho;* yourself - *ia oe iho;* himself - *iaia iho.*

When one speaks of himself, the motion is neither away from nor toward him but downward, so he uses *iho*. The same applies to yourself and himself.

Iho is also the verb to descend and the directive *aku* or *mai* may be used with it.

When a person says *"E iho aku oe,"* he means to go down, away from him. If he says, *"E iho mai oe,"* he means to come down toward him.

Therefore, the directives *a'e* and *iho* are not used when the motion is away from or toward the speaker, although the direction be upward or downward. In such case, the directive *aku* or *mai* is used.

Whenever the directive is omitted, the action is understood to be away from the speaker.

Note: The first *a* in the word *ala* is dropped when it follows any of the directives and *la* is joined to the directive as, *maila, akula, a'ela* and *ihola.*

Vocabulary
Verbs with Directives Aku and Mai

ae aku - to agree to that, to agree with him, to consent to him, to permit him

ae mai - to agree to this, to agree with me, to consent to me, to permit me

a'o aku - to teach him

a'o mai - to teach me

iho aku - to descend that way, to go down

iho mai - to descend this way, to come down

ike aku - to see that, to see him, to perceive that

ike mai - to see this, to see me, to perceive this

olelo aku - to say to him, to speak to him, to tell him

olelo mai - to say to me, to speak to me, to tell me

heluhelu aku - to read that, to read to him

heluhelu mai - to read this, to read to me

holo aku - to run toward him, to sail that way

holo mai - to run toward me, to sail this way

Kahea aku - to call him, to call to them

kahea mai - to call me, to call to me

kuai aku - to buy that, to sell that; to sell to him

kuai mai - to buy this, to sell to me

nana aku - to look at him, to look that way

nana mai - to look at me, to look this way

ninau aku - to ask him a question

ninau mai - to ask me a question

noi aku - to ask him for something, to ask his permission

noi mai - to ask me for something, to ask my permission

pane aku - to answer him

pane mai - to answer me

pii aku - to climb up there, to go up there

pii mai - to climb up here, to come up here

Exercise

Read and translate into English

I. E kahea aku oe i na kanaka. 2. E nana aku oe i na papale. 3. E heluhelu mai oe i ka puke. 4. E pane mai oe i ke kumukula. 5. E holo mai olua. 6. E kuai aku olua i na kuka. 7. E pii aku olua. 8. E iho mai oukou. 9. E heluhelu aku oe i ka nupepa. 10. E aʻo aku oe i na keiki.

Translate into Hawaiian

1. Call to the men. 2. Look at the hat. 3. Read the newspaper. 4. Answer the teacher. 5. Run to the school. 6. Sell the coat. 7. Buy the shoe. 8. You (more than two) go down. 9. Look at the boy and the girl. 10. Teach the child.

HAAWINA UMIKUMAMAWALU
(Lesson Eighteen)

Ihea aku nei oe? - Where have you been?
Where did you go?
I Halawa aku nei au. - I have been to Halawa
I went to Halawa
I Honolulu aku nei au. - I have been to Honolulu.
I went to Honolulu.
I ka halawai aku nei au. - I have been to the meeting.
I went to the meeting.

CONJUGATION OF VERBS

The natural division of tense in the Hawaiian Language is present, past and future.

Hawaiian verbs do not change to form tenses. Separate little words combined with verbs form tenses. They may precede the verb or precede and follow the verb in the sentence.

Present Tense

The present tense is made by placing *ke* before the verb and *nei* after the same verb; as, *ke hana nei au* - I work. This word combination indicates that the action is taking place while the person speaks.

We shall call this form of *nei* the tense suffix.

However, when a directive is used, *nei* follows the directive.

For example:

Ke lawe aku nei na keiki i na apala - The children take the apples.

Ke lawe mai nei na keiki i ko lakou mau pokii - The children bring their younger brothers and sisters.

Note: The particle *ke* prefixed to verbs as shown above must not be confused with the definite article *ke*.

Conjugation of nana (nah nah') - to look

PRESENT TENSE

Singular

Ke nana nei au - I look

Ke nana aku nei au - I look (that way)

Ke nana nei oe - you look

Ke nana mai nei oe - you look (this way or toward me)

Ke nana nei oia - he/she looks

Ke nana aku nei oia - he/she looks (that way or away from me)

Ke nana mai nei oia - he/she looks (this way or toward me)

Ke nana nei oiala - he/she (over there) looks

Ke nana mai nei oiala - he/she (over there) looks (this way)

Ke nana aku nei oinei - he/she (over here) looks (that way)

Dual (Two)

Ke nana nei kaua - we (you and I) look

Ke nana nei maua - we (he/she and I) look

Ke nana nei olua - you (two) look

Ke nana nei laua - they (two) look

Ke nana nei laua ala - they (two over there) look

Ke nana nei laua nei - they (two over here) look

Plural (more than two)

Ke nana nei kakou - we (you, he/she/they and I) look
Ke nana nei makou - we (he/she/they and I) look
Ke nana nei oukou - you (more than two) look
Ke nana nei lakou - they (more than two) look
Ke nana nei lakou ala - they (more than two over there) look
Ke nana nei lakou nei - they (more than two over here) look

A variation of action is the use of *ala* in place of *nei*. This implies that the action is in the present tense but is taking place elsewhere for *ala* (there) is the opposite of *nei* (here); as, *ke holo ala lakou i ka moana* - they are now sailing out there on the ocean.

The first *a* in the word *ala* is dropped when it follows a directive, and *la* is joined to the directive; as,

aʻe and *ala* become *aʻela*
aku and *ala* become *akula*
mai and *ala* become *maila*, and
iho and *ala* become *ihola*

For example:

ke nee aʻela na kanaka iuka - the men move inland, toward the
                               mountain.
ua pae akula lakou - they have landed somewhere out there.
ke holo maila lakou - they are now sailing this way.
lele ihola na keiki ilalo - the children jumped down.

PAST TENSE

The past tense is formed by prefixing *ua*. However, when a verbal directive is used, *nei* must follow the directive; as, *ua hele mai nei oia* - she came.

Aku nei and *mai nei* after a verb preceded by *ua,* may express the distinction of the perfect tense; as, *ua hana aku nei au* - I worked; I have worked.

Singular

ua nana au - I looked
  ua nana aku nei au - I looked (that way)
ua nana oe - you looked
  ua nana mai nei* oe - you looked (this way)
ua nana oia - he/she looked
  ua nana aku nei oia - he/she looked (that way)
  ua nana mai nei oia - he/she looked (this way)
ua nana oiala - he/she (over there) looked
ua nana oinei - he/she (over here) looked
  ua nana aku nei oinei - he/she (over here) looked (that way)
  ua nana mai nei oinei - he/she (over here) looked (this way)

Dual (two)

ua nana kaua - we (you and I) looked
ua nana maua - we (he/she and I) looked
ua nana olua - you (two) looked
ua nana laua - they (two) looked
ua nana laua ala - they (two over there) looked
ua nana laua nei - they (two over here) looked

Plural (more than two)

ua nana kakou - we (you, he/she/they and I) looked
ua nana makou - we (he/she/they and I) looked
ua nana oukou - you (more than two) looked
ua nana lakou - they (more than two) looked
ua nana lakou ala - they (more than two over there) looked
ua nana lakou nei - they (more than two over here) looked

---

* *nei* also follows the directive when it is used in the dual and plural numbers.

FUTURE TENSE

The future tense is formed by placing *e* before the verb, and adding one of the directives *aku* or *mai* and the tense suffix *ana* after the verb.

Both directives cannot be used together with the same verb.

Singular

e nana aku ana au - I shall look
e nana aku ana oe - you will look
e nana aku ana oia - he/she will look
e nana aku ana oiala - he/she (over there) will look
e nana aku ana oinei - he/she (over here) will look

Dual (two)

e nana aku ana kaua - we (you and I) shall look
e nana aku ana maua - we (he/she and I) shall look
e nana aku ana olua - you (two) will look
e nana aku ana laua - they (two) will look
e nana aku ana laua ala - they (two over there) will look
e nana aku ana laua nei - they (two over here) will look

Plural (more than two)

e nana aku ana kakou - we (you, he/she/they and I) shall look
e nana aku ana makou - we (he/she/they and I) shall look
e nana aku ana oukou - you (more than two) will look
e nana aku ana lakou - they (more than two) will look
e nana aku ana lakou ala - they (more than two over there) will look
e nana aku ana lakou nei - they (more than two over here) will look

PROGRESSIVE FORM

In English, such verb forms as, I am working *(e hana ana au);* they were eating *(e ai ana lakou);* you will be singing *(e himeni ana oe)* are used instead of I work *(ke hana nei au);* they ate *(ua ai lakou)* and you will sing *(e himeni aku ana oe)*. They are formed by the use of the verb "to be" with the present participle of another verb as, is going *(e hele ana)*, was going *(e hele ana)* and will be going *(e hele ana)*. This form, I am working, they were eating, etc. is called the progressive form because it represents the action in progress or continuing.

Since there is no equivalent for the verb "to be" in the Hawaiian language, only the present participle of the verb expresses the progressive form. This is made by using *e* before the verb and *ana* after the same verb.

Ana may be separated from the verb by any qualifying word or phrase; as, *E kukulu hale ana oia* - he is house building; he is building a house; *E kuʻi ai ana lakou* - they (more than two) are poi pounding, or - they (more than two) are pounding poi.

Since the use of *e* and *ana* does not indicate clearly whether the progressive tense is past, present or future, other words and phrases are added.

For example:
E himeni ana au ia manawa - I was singing at that time
E himeni ana au i kona wa i hiki mai ai - I was singing at the time he
                    arrived; I was singing when he arrived
E himeni ana makou i keia pule aʻe - We will be singing next week

The addition of the phrases *ia manawa* (at that time), *i kona wa i hiki mai ai* (at the time of his arrival) and *i keia pule aʻe* (next week) determine the time of the progressive action.

Singular
e nana ana au - I am looking
e nana ana oe - you are looking
e nana ana oia - he/she is looking
e nana ana oiala - he/she (over there) is looking
e nana ana oinei - he/she (over here) is looking

Dual (two)
e nana ana kaua - we (you and I) are looking
e nana ana maua - we (he/she and I) are looking

e nana ana olua - you (two) are looking
e nana ana laua - they (two) are looking
e nana ana laua ala - they (two over there) are looking
e nana ana laua nei - they (two over here) are looking

Review

Read and translate into English

1. Ka elemakule, ka luahine, ke kanaka ame ka wahine. 2. Ke kaikaina, ke kaikuaana, ke kaikuahine ame ka makuakane. 3. Ke kaikamahine, ke keikikane ame ka luahine. 4. Ka pahi, ke o ame na puna. 5. Ka makuakane, ka makuahine ame ke keiki. 6. Ka puke, na haawina ame ke kumukula. 7. Ka ipuhao, ka wahie ame ke ahi. 8. Ke kanaka, ka noho ame ka nupepa. 9. Ua kahea aku nei makou. 10. E heluhelu mai ana lakou.

Translate into Hawaiian

1. The mother, the father and the daughter. 2. The dress, the hat and the coat. 3. The home, the husband and the wife. 4. The older brother, the younger brother, the sister and the father. 5. The ink, the pen and the paper. 6. The dish, knife, fork and spoon. 7. The pot, wood and fire. 8. The man is calling (to us). 9. The teacher will teach (them). 10. The children asked (us) a question.

HAAWINA UMIKUMAMAIWA
(Lesson Nineteen)

THE CAUSATIVE PREFIX

Hoo is a causative prefix used with some verbs to express action which causes result. There are a great many verbs in the Hawaiian language which are not active. They are in a state of existence and contain the verb "to be". They cannot be used in sentences in the active voice without the causative prefix *"hoo"* to make them active, as: *ua paa ka haawina* - the lesson is learned; *ua hoopaa au i ka haawina* - I studied the lesson; *ua moʻa ka iʻa* -the fish is cooked; *ua hoomoʻa au i ka iʻa* - I cooked the fish.

They can only be used in sentences in the passive voice.

Vocabulary

a - to be burning, as a fire or lamp

hoʻa - to light, as a fire or lamp

akaaka - to be clear; to be distinct; to be plain

hooakaaka - to explain; to make clear

ala - to be awake

hooala - to waken someone; to

rouse someone

iliili - an accumulation; a mass or heap; a large quantity; a pile, to be accumulated

hoʻiliili - to accumulate; to heap; to pile; to save

akea - to be wide or broad; to be large; to be roomy

hooakea - to broaden or widen; to enlarge

alu - to be slack, as a rope or wire

hoʻalu - to slacken

ili - to be vested in; to be derived; to be inherited; to fall or come to one, as an inheritance

hooili - to devise; to will; to bequeath or leave in a will

oia - to be true; to be correct

hooia - to affirm; to assent; to admit; to confirm; to profess; to make evident; to acknowledge

oiaiʻo - truth, proof

hooiaiʻo - to acknowledge to verify; to confirm; to substantiate; to testify; to attest; to prove

hauʻoli - to be happy; to be merry; to be joyful; to rejoice

hoohauʻoli - to cause to be happy; to make happy; to bring happiness; to bring joy

apono - to be approved; to be accepted; to be justified

hoʻapono - to approve; to accept; to justify

eha - to be hurt; to be sore; to be in pain

hoʻeha - to hurt someone; to cause pain

emi - to be decreased in number or size; to be less; to be cheap

hoʻemi - to decrease in number or size; to lessen; to reduce, to diminish

kau - to be on some designated place; to be in an elevated situation

hookau - to put on some designated place

lako - to be supplied; to be provided; to be furnished

hoolako - to supply; to provide; to furnish

like - to be alike; to be similar; to be even; to be equal

hoohalike - to match; to make similar

hoolike - to make even; to divide equally

maa - to be accustomed; to become accustomed

hoomaa - to accustom; to make one accustomed; to practice

makaʻu - to be afraid; to be frightened

hoomakaʻu - to scare; to frighten

makaukau - to be ready; to be prepared

hoomakaukau - to make ready; to prepare

paa - to be fastened; to be secured; to be tight; to be completed; to be bound; to be learned

hoopaa - to fasten; to bind; to tighten; to make secure; to complete; to detain; to learn; to study

Before words which begin with a vowel, the last *o* of *hoo* is frequently dropped for the sake of euphony, as *hoʻalu* (to slacken)

instead of *hoo alu; ho'emi* (to reduce) instead of *hoo emi; ho'apono* (to approve) instead of *hoo apono.*

Some words have *haa* for causative prefixes instead of *hoo,* as *haalele* (to leave) and *haanui* (to exaggerate, to boast).

Exercise

Read and translate into English

1. Ua akaaka na haawina ia kakou. 2. Ke hooakaaka nei o Keoni i ka haawina. 3. Ua akea ka lumi hookipa. 4. Ua hooakea au i ka lumi aina. 5. Ua eha ke keiki ia oe. 6. Ua ho'eha mai oe ia'u. 7. Ua makaukau ka mea ai no oukou. 8. E hoomakaukau aku ana makou i ka mea ai. 9. Ua paa na haawina i na haumana. 10. Ke hoopaa nei o Iokepa i na haawina. 11. Ua ala o Mele. 12. Ua hooala aku nei o Keoni ia Mele.

Translate into Hawaiian

1. The girl is frightened. 2. John scared the girl. 3. The boat is fastened. 4. We fastened the boat. 5. The lesson is learned by the pupils. 6. We will all study the lessons. 7. We are happy to see all of you. 8. The children are making us happy. 9. The girl is hurt by you. 10. You hurt those children. 11. The children are awake. 12. The man will awaken the children.

HAAWINA IWAKALUA
(Lesson Twenty)

OTHER VERBS REQUIRING THE CAUSATIVE PREFIX

There are other verbs which are active, but the action must be performed by the person addressed; as, *e nee mai oe* - you move (yourself) this way; *ua ike o Malia i ka hale* - Maria saw the house. In order for someone to cause the action, it is necessary to use the causative prefix *hoo*; as, *e hoonee mai oe i ka noho* - move the chair this way. *Ua ho'ike mai o Malia i ka hale ia'u* - Maria showed me the house (Maria caused me to see the house). *Ke holo ala ka mokuahi i ka moana* - the steamer is sailing out there on the ocean. *Ke hooholo ala o Keoni i ka mokuahi i ka moana* - John sails the steamer out there on the ocean. *Ke lele maila ka lupe iluna o ka lani* - the kite flies in the sky. *Ke hoolele maila o Iokepa i ka lupe* - Joseph flies the kite.

Vocabulary

akaaka - to laugh

ho'akaaka - to make others laugh; to bring laughter

ike - to see; to perceive; to know; to understand

ho'ike - to cause one to see; to show; to enlighten someone; to exhibit; to make known, to make plain; to relate to some-one

holo - to run; to sail; to ride; as in a car

hooholo - to run as an engine; to sail a boat; to drive a car

nee - to move one's self

hoonee - to move someone or something

Exercise

Read and Translate into English

1. Ke akaaka nei na wahine. 2. Ke ho'akaaka mai nei o Keaka i na wahine. 3. Ua ike mai nei o Mele i keia puke. 4. E ho'ike aku ana au i keia puke ia Mele. 5. Ke holo nei ka waapa i ke kai. 6. Ke hooholo nei o Keo i ka waapa. 7. Ua nee aku nei o Makaleka. 8. E hoonee aku ana lakou i ke pakaukau.

Translate into Hawaiian

1. Margaret saw the book. 2. I showed her the book. 3. The girls will laugh at us. 4. Jack will make the girls laugh. 5. The boat is sailing on the sea. 6. George sailed the boat. 7. The children will move (this way). 8. We moved the chair (that way).

Vocabulary of Verbs

ai - to eat (modern usage, based on the Hawaiian word *ai,* meaning food)

a'o - to learn; to teach

oki - to cut

haawi - to give

ho'i (aku) - to return (there or that way); to go back; to go home

ho'i mai - to return (here or this way); to come back; to come home

ho'iho'i (aku) - to return something (to him); to take back

ho'iho'i mai - to return something (to me); to bring back

hoopaa - to fasten; to study

hoopaa naau - to memorize; to study well; to learn well (literal - to fasten to the intestines)

kakau - to write

koi - to urge; to compel; to ask (ask or invite one to go in company with him; ask a favor)

ku'ai - to buy; to sell

moku - to be cut

ninau - to ask, as information; to inquire; to interrogate

noi - to ask (permission); to request (ask for a thing)

paa - to be tight; to be fastened; to be closed; to be covered

paa naau - to be well learned; to be memorized

pa'ina - to eat; partake of food

pani - to close or shut, as a door

wehe - to open, as a door

Exercise

Read and translate into English

1. Ke a'o nei au ia oe. 2. Ua ho'iho'i aku nei au i ka penikala. 3. E ho'i mai ana o Keoni. 4. Ke hoopaanaau nei o Mele i ka haawina. 5. Ua kakau aku nei makou i ka leka. 6. E kuai aku ana maua i ka aina. 7. Ke pani nei o Keoki i ka puke. 8. Ua wehe aku nei lakou i ka puka aniani. 9. E kii aku ana o Iokepa i ke kanake. 10. Ke lawe nei au i ke pakaukau.

Translate into Hawaiian

1. I will open the door. 2. John closed the window. 3. She taught me the lessons. 4. Mary buys the book. 5. He and I write the lesson. 6. George will memorize the lesson. 7. Joseph went home. 8. They returned the pencil. 9. You and I shall take her to school. 10. They sold the dresses.

HAAWINA IWAKALUAKUMAMAKAHI
(Lesson Twenty-one)

PERSONAL PRONOUNS
Objective Case

The prepositions *i* and *ia* (both meaning to) are the objective signs that designate the direction of the action. They must be used before the object inasmuch as all Hawaiian verbs have motion. The preposition *i* is used before common nouns and names of places, and *ia* is used before pronouns and names of persons.

When a sentence contains both the direct and the indirect objects, the direct object precedes the indirect object.

For example:
Ua lawe mai nei na wahine i na keiki i ke kula - The women brought the children to school.
Ke ho'ike mai nei na kaikamahine i na lole ia kakou - The girls are showing us the dresses.
E ha'i aku ana au i ka mea hou ia Keoni - I will tell John the news.
E a'o aku ana ke kumukula i na haawina i na haumana - The teacher will teach the lessons to the pupils.

Ke lawe nei na makua i na keiki i ke kula - The parents are taking the children to school.
Ua ho‘iho‘i mai nei na kanaka i ka mea ai i kauhale - The men brought the food home.

Singular

ia‘u - me, to me
ia oe - you, to you
iaia - her, to her; him, to him
iaiala - her/him (over there), to her/him (over there)
iainei - her/him (over here), to her/him (over here)

Dual (Two)

ia kaua - us (you and me), to us (you and me)
ia maua - us (him/her and me), to us (him/her and me)
ia olua - you (two), to you (two)
ia laua - them (two), to them (two)
ia laua ala - them (two over there), to them (two over there)
ia laua nei - them (two over here), to them (two over here)

Plural (More than two)

ia kakou - us (you, him/her/them and me), to us (you, him/her/them and me).
ia makou - us (him/her/them and me), to us (him/her/them and me)
ia oukou - you (more than two), to you (more than two)
ia lakou - them (more than two), to them (more than two)
ia lakou ala - them (more than two over there), to them (more than two over there)
ia lakou nei - them (more than two over here), to them (more than two over here)

Oral Drill

oia, ia kaua, ia oukou, ia laua ala, ia lakou, ia maua, ia inei, ia'u, ia kakou, ia lakou nei, iaia, ia laua, iaiala, ia maua, ia oe, ia lakou ala, ia makou, ia olua, ia laua nei, au, ia'u, oe, ia oe, oia, iaia, kaua, ia kaua, ia maua, maua, ia olua, olua, ia laua, laua, laua ala, ia laua ala, laua nei, ia laua nei.

us, (them and me); him, to them (more than two over there); to you; to us (him and me); them (two over here); us (you and me); to you (two); him, (over here); us (you, her and me); them (two); him (over there); me; to you (more than two); them (more than two over here); you and me; to them (more than two); to them (two over there); I; me; you; to you; he; him; she; her; you and I; you and me; you (two); to you (two); he and I; him and me; you (two); to you (two); they (two); them (two); they (two over there); they (two over here).

Vocabulary

i - to (before common nouns and names of places)

ia - to (before pronouns and names of persons)

Vocabulary of Nouns

ke kakini - the stocking
ke kala - the dollar, the money
ke kumulaau - the tree

ka leka - the letter

ka pa - the fence
ka puka - the door, the hole
ka puka pa - the gate
ka pukaaniani - the window
ka wai - the water

Vocabulary of Verbs

ai - to eat

inu - to drink

oki - to cut

hele - to go

hele mai - to come

helu - to count

kahi - to comb

kakau - to write

kali - to wait

kokua - to assist, to help

lele - to fly

noho - to sit, to live, to reside

pani - to close

wehe - to open

Exercise

Read and translate into English

1. Ke kali nei oinei ia lakou ala. 2. Ua kakau maua i ka leka ia oe. 3. E kokua aku oukou i na elemakule. 4. E pani aku ana ke kanaka i ka puka pa. 5. Ke oki nei ka makuakane i ka wahie. 6. Ua wehe na keiki i na pukaaniani. 7. E aʻo aku ana makou ia oukou. 8. Ua inu laua ala i ka wai. 9. Ke kahea mai nei ke kumukula ia kakou. 10. Ke helu nei na wahine i ke kala.

Translate into Hawaiian

1. The children closed the windows. 2. They (two over there) are writing the letters to us (you, them and me). 3. We (they and I) will wait for them (more than two over there). 4. The men are closing the gates. 5. We (she and I) will teach you (two). 6. You (more than two) help the old women. 7. He (over there) is drinking the water. 8. The fathers counted the money. 9. The old man will cut the wood. 10. The teacher called you (two).

HAAWINA IWAKALUAKUMAMALUA
(Lesson Twenty-two)

SENTENCES

Most Hawaiian sentences begin with the predicate, followed by the subject and then the object.

The usual order of simple Hawaiian sentences is:
1. The tense prefixes, *ke, ua, e*
2. The verb
3. The verbal directives *aku, mai,* etc.
4. The tense suffix *nei* or *ana*
5. The subject
6. The particles of direction, *ala* or *nei*
7. The objective sign *i* or *ia*
8. The object

In the sentence *ke lawe mai nei laua ala i ka lio* - they (two, over there) are bringing the horse:
1. *ke* is the tense prefix
2. *lawe* is the verb

3. *mai* is the verbal directive
4. *nei* is the tense suffix
5. *laua* is the subject
6. *ala* is the particle of direction
7. *i* is the objective sign, and
8. *lio* is the object

When the name of a person is the subject of a sentence, it requires the "*o* emphatic." There is no part of speech that corresponds with it in the English language; nor is there a word into which it can be translated. It is, however, of great importance in Hawaiian for emphasis and euphony. The "*o* emphatic" usually stands immediately before the subject. It is only used before names of persons.

In the sentence David will show them the picture - *e hoʻike aku ana o Kawika i ke kii ia lakou:*

e is the tense prefix
hoʻike is the verb
aku is the verbal directive
ana is the tense suffix
o is the "o emphatic"
Kawika is the subject
i and *ia* are the objective signs
kii is the direct object, and
lakou is the indirect object

Vocabulary of Hawaiianized English names

Aukake - August
Ana - Anna
Elena - Ellen
Hanale - Henry
Heneli - Henri, Henry
Kale - Charles, Charlie
Kalela - Clara
Kaniela - Daniel

Kawika - David
Keaka - Jack
Kulia - Julia
Lopaka - Robert
Luka - Ruth
Maka - Martha
Moke - Moses

Vocabulary of nouns

ka ilio - the dog

ka ipukukui - the lamp; the light

ke kaa - the car

ke kii - the doll, the picture

ka lepo - the dirt

ka moolelo - the history, the story

ke pooleka - the stamp

ka popoki - the cat

ka waapa - the boat, the skiff

ka wahileka - the envelope

Vocabulary of verbs

haawi - to give, to grant

ha'i - to recite, to relate, to tell a story

ho'a - to light as a fire or a lamp

ho'ike - to show

kii, kii aku - to fetch, to go and get

kii mai - to come and get

kinai - to put out as a light or fire, to extinguish, to quench

koi - to ask, to invite, to urge

laka - to lock

lawe, lawe aku - to take

lawe mai - to bring

nahu - to bite

Exercise

Read and translate into English

1. Ke koi aku nei o Kale ia Lopaka e hele mai. 2. E haawi aku ana o Keala i ka waapa ia lakou. 3. Ua kii aku nei o Kawika i ke kaa. 4. E ha'i aku ana au i ka moolelo ia Aukake. 5. Ua lawe mai nei o Kaniela i na wahileka. 6. Ke ho'ike nei laua i ke kii ia Luka. 7. E ho'a aku ana o Elena i ka ipukukui. 8. Ke lawe aku nei o Moke i na noho. 9. Ua nahu ka ilio i ke kanaka. 10. E kii mai ana o Ana i ka popoki.

Translate into Hawaiian

1. Robert is lighting the lamps. 2. I showed August the

pictures. 3. David brought the stamps to us. 4. Daniel will go and get the chairs. 5. Charles is telling you (two) the story. 6. Ellen gave you (more than two) the envelopes. 7. Moses is asking Ruth to come. 8. The dog bit the man. 9. Jack will come to get the car. 10. Henry took the boat to them.

Fill in the blanks, read and translate

1. Ke heluhelu aku nei ＿＿＿＿＿ kanaka ＿＿＿＿＿

＿＿＿＿＿ moolelo ＿＿＿＿＿oe.

2. E hoʻike mai ana ＿＿＿＿＿ Kale ＿＿＿＿＿ ＿＿＿＿＿

Kii ＿＿＿＿＿ makou.

3. Ua kahea aku nei ＿＿＿＿＿ Luka ＿＿＿＿＿ Aukake.

4. Ke pani nei ＿＿＿＿＿ wahine ＿＿＿＿＿ ＿＿＿＿＿

pukaaniani.

5. Ua lawe mai nei ＿＿＿＿＿ Moke ＿＿＿＿＿ ＿＿＿＿＿

waapa.

6. Ke haʻi mai nei ＿＿＿＿＿ Elena ＿＿＿＿＿ ＿＿＿＿＿

moolelo ＿＿＿＿＿ kakou.

7. Ua hoʻa aku nei ＿＿＿＿＿ Lopaka ＿＿＿＿＿ ＿＿＿＿＿

ipukukui.

HAAWINA IWAKALUAKUMAMAKOLU
(Lesson Twenty-three)

THE IMPERATIVE MOOD

The imperative mood expresses a command or a request. Sentences in the imperative mood begin with *e.*

Examples:

E hoʻi mai oe! - Come back! Come home!

E pani aku oe i ka puka! - Close the door!

E hoolohe mai oe! - Listen!

The subject is rarely omitted in the imperative mood.

When addressing someone in a command, *e* appears before the name of the person as well as before the verb.

Examples:

E Keoni, e pani aku oe i ka puka! - John, close the door!

E Mele, e wehe mai oe i keia puka aniani! - Mary, open this window!

When expressing a wish such as, Let us sing, we say, *E himeni kakou.*

Mai is the negative of the imperative mood and is used in place of *e.*

Examples:

Mai lawe aku oe i kena puke. - Do not take that book.

E Makaleka, mai hooala aku oe i kela kaikamahine liilii. -
Margaret, do not waken that little girl.

Exercise

Read and translate into English

1. E Keoni, e heluhelu mai oe i keia moolelo ia'u. 2. E ho'iho'i aku olua i keia mau popoki i kela luahine. 3. E Kaniela, mai ai oe i kena mau manako. 4. E Kale, e hanai aku oe i ka ilio. 5. E Elena, e lawe mai oe i kela mau pua. 6. E Luka, mai komo oe i kena lole. 7. E Kawika, e kahea aku oe ia Makaleka e ho'i mai. 8. E kokua aku oukou i kela po'e elemakule. 9. E Moke, mai lawe aku oe i ka puke i ke kula. 10. E haawi mai olua i kena mau kala ia maua.

Translate into Hawaiian

1. Daniel, take that book to the teacher. 2. You (more than two) help those old women. 3. You (two) do not wait for us (two). 4. Moses, read this story to those children. 5. Take these cats back to that old woman. 6. John, do not eat that mango. 7. Ruth, call David to come home. 8. Charles, feed this dog. 9. Ellen, do not wear that dress. 10. David, bring those flowers to me.

HAAWINA IWAKALUAKUMAMAHA
(Lesson Twenty-four)

DESCRIPTIVE ADJECTIVES

Words used to modify or describe nouns are called adjectives as, *na kamaa ula'ula* - red shoes; *na wawae liilii* - small feet; *hale laau* - wooden house.

They always follow the nouns they describe. There is no exception to this rule.

There are three degrees of comparison in Hawaiian descriptive adjectives: Positive, comparative, and superlative.

Adjectives are compared by adding *ike a'e* or by prefixing *oi a'e ka* or *oi aku ka* for the comparative and prefixing *ka* and adding *loa* for the superlative.

Whenever it is necessary to compare adjectives to indicate less of the quality instead of more, the directive *iho* is used in place of *a'e* and *mai* in place of *aku*.

Positive	Comparative	Superlative
u'i - pretty	*u'i iki a'e* - a little prettier *oi a'e ka u'i* - prettier *oi aku ka u'i* - prettier	*ka u'i loa* - prettiest
maika'i - good	*maika'i iki a'e* - a little better *oi a'e ka maika'i* - better *oi aku ka maika'i* - better	*ka maika'i loa* - best
nui - big	*nui iki a'e* - a little bigger *oi a'e ka nui* - bigger *oi aku ka nui* - bigger	*ka nui loa* - biggest
uuku - small	*uuku iki iho* - a little smaller *oi iho ka uuku* - smaller *oi mai ka uuku* - smaller	*ka uuku loa* - smallest

Note: *Loa* used after the adjective, without the definite article, usually means "too", as *uuku loa keia* - this is too small;this is too little; *nui loa kela* - that is too big; that is too much.

Examples:

Uuku loa keia hale no oukou - this house is too small for you.

Nui loa kena mea ono, aole e pau ana ia oe - that cake is too big, you cannot finish it.

He nui o Keoni - John is big.

He nui iki a'e kona kaikaina, o Moke - his younger brother, Moses, is a little bigger.

O ko laua kaikuaana na'e, o Uiliama, ka mea nui loa o lakou - but their oldest brother, William, is the biggest of them.

He uuku o Kalela - Clara is small.

He uuku iki iho o Luka, kona kaikuaana - Ruth, her older sister,is a little smaller.

O ko laua kaikaina na'e, o Elena, ka mea uuku loa o lakou ekolu - but their younger sister, Ellen, is the smallest of the three.

When comparing one object with another or one person with another, the word "than" is expressed by *mamua o,* as: Mary is older than Jean - *He nui aku ko Mele mau makahiki mamua o Kini.* This apple is sweeter than that - *He oi aku ka momona o keia apala mamua o kena.*

Vocabulary

aala - fragrant, perfumed, sweet-scented

akamai - skillful, smart

ako - to pick, to pluck, as flowers or fruit

ala - fragrant, perfumed, sweet-scented

eleele - black

opiopio - young

uʻi - beautiful, handsome, pretty

ulaʻula - red

ka hale kula - the school building, the school house

hana - to do, to fix, to make, to work

hanai - to feed

himeni - to sing

hoʻi aku - go back, go home

hoʻi mai - come back, come home

hoʻihoʻi aku - to return to him, to take back

hoʻihoʻi mai - to return to me, to bring back

hou - new, again

hou - to pierce, to poke, to prick

honi - to kiss, to smell, as a flower

ke kaimana - Hawaiian for diamond

ke kaona - Hawaiian for town

kahiko - old

keʻokeʻo - white

Keoni - John, Johnny

Kimo - James, Jim, Jimmy

kolohe - bad, dishonest, mischievous, naughty

komo - to wear, to enter

ke komo - the ring

Exercise

Read and translate into English

1. Ke oki nei na keiki kolohe i na kumulaau nui. 2. Ua nana aku nei o Keoki i na home kahiko. 3. E lawe mai ana ke kaikamahine i na lole ulaʻula nani. 4. Ua kuai mai nei o Mele i na komo kaimana uʻi. 5. Ke kinai nei na keiki akamai i ke ahi. 6. E hoʻike hou mai oe i ke kaa eleele ia maua. 7. Ke paani nei o Kulia me na popoki keʻokeʻo uuku. 8. E Iokepa e helu aku oe i na noho kahiko. 9. Ua hoʻa aku nei makou i na ipukukui liilii, e nana aku oukou. 10. Ua aʻo aku nei na kumukula akamai i na kamalii opiopio. 11. Oi aku ka ike o koʻu kumukula mamua o kou. 12. He uuku iho koʻu kaikunane mamua o kou kaikuahine. 13. Oi aku ka uʻi o ke kaikamahine a Keoki mamua o kou kaikuahine. 14. He oi

aku ka maikai o kou peni mamua o ko'u, aka, he oi aku ka maikai o
ko'u penikala mamua o kou. 15. He nui a'e ka lumi aina o ko makou
home mamua o kou. 16. He oi a'e ka loihi o kou kaikunane mamua
o'u. 17. Aole anei he opiopio iki oia mamua o'u? 18. Ae, he opiopio
iki iho oia mamua ou.

Translate into Hawaiian

1. Clara will return the pretty red dresses to them (more than
two). 2. Julia fed the little black cats. 3. George bought the big red
house. 4. The naughty boys have cut the little trees. 5. John wore
the new white coat. 6. James brought back the old table. 7. The
smart men are building the new homes. 8. The old men are
teaching the young men. 9. The young children will come to the
new school. 10. The old women picked the fragrant flowers. 11.
The dining room of our home is smaller than the kitchen. 12. Your
pen is better than mine, but my pencil is better than yours. 13.
Your brother is taller than my sister. 14. My sister is prettier than
John's daughter. 15. My father is shorter than you. 16. Is he not
younger than you? 17. Yes, he is younger than I am. 18. My
teacher is smarter than yours.

HAAWINA IWAKALUAKUMAMALIMA
(Lesson Twenty-five)

SIMPLE PREPOSITIONS

In Hawaiian there are simple and compound prepositions. The simple prepositions are:

A - until, of

Ua kali makou a ka Poaha - We waited until Thursday.
Ke keiki keia a kela wahine - This is the son of that woman.

E - by

E hoomakaukau ia ana ka mea ai e kela kaikamahine - The food will be prepared by that girl.

I - in, at, to, for

Ke noho nei o Mele i Kauai - Mary is living in Kauai.
E haalele ana kakou i ka hola eha - We shall leave at four o'clock.
Ua hele aku nei lakou i ka pule - They went to church.
E huli aku oe i ke ki - Look for the key.

Ia - to, by, for, about

Ua kuʻai mai nei o Keoki i ke kaa ia makou - George sold the car to us.

Ua haawi aku nei makou i na lole ia Peke - We gave the dresses to Betty.

Ua loaa ka apolima ia Akeneki - The bracelet was found by Agnes.

Ke kali nei makou ia Makaleka - We are waiting for Margaret.

E pono kakou e noonoo ia lakou - We must think about them.

O - of

O ka makuakane kela o keia keiki - That is the father of this boy.

Ma - by, on, at, along

Ke ku mai nei oia ma kela noho - She is standing by that chair.

Ua waiho aku nei au i ka puʻolo ma ka pakaukau - I left the package on the table.

Ke paani mai nei kamalii ma kahakai - The children are playing at the beach.

Ke holo nei ka palena o keia aina ma ka papohaku - The boundary of this land runs along the stone wall.

Mai - from (the directives *aku* or *mai* are required after the name of place)

Ua hele mai nei keia poʻe wahine mai Hawaii mai - These women came from Hawaii.

Ua hele aku nei kela poʻe kanaka mai Oahu aku - Those men went from Oahu.

Me - with

Ua hele mai nei oia me na keiki - She came with the children.

Na - for

Ke hoomakaukau nei o Mina i mea ai na oukou apau - Mina is preparing food for all of you.

No - for

E Keoki, e lawe mai oe i noho no makou - George, bring chairs for us.

Exercise

Read and translate into English

1. Ua loaa na komo kaimana ia Makaleka. 2. Ke kaikamahine keia a ko'u kaikunane. 3. E kali aku ana makou ia oe a ka hola ekolu. 4. Ua hoomakaukau ia ka lumi moe no kakou. 5. Ke noho mai nei o Aukake i Maui i keia manawa. 6. E hiki aku ana makou i ka hola elima. 7. Ua hele aku nei na keiki a maua i ka pule. 8. E Leimana, e haawi aku oe i ka upena ia Alape. 9. Ua ho'iho'i aku nei o Lopaka i na keiki me ia. 10. Ke lawe mai nei o Mina i noho no Aukake.

Translate into Hawaiian

1. They will arrive here at two o'clock. 2. They waited for us until three o'clock. 3. The children will go to church today. 4. The diamond ring was found by Agnes. 5. The room was made ready by the students. 6. Raymond is giving the boat to Ellen. 7. This is the son of my brother. 8. Robert will bring the children with him. 9. Mina, bring a chair for Andrew. 10. Margaret now lives on Oahu.

HAAWINA IWAKALUAKUMAMAONO
(Lesson Twenty-six)

COMPOUND PREPOSITIONS

The compound prepositions are made up of the simple prepositions (Lesson 25) and words denoting place.

luna - up
lalo - down
mua - front
hope - back

loko - in
waho - out
waena - mid or middle

The compound prepositions are:

Iluna - up (denotes motion upward)
> *Ua pii aku nei ka po'e koa iluna o na alapii* -The soldier climbed up the ladders.

Maluna - on, above
> *Ua waiho aku nei makou i na puolo maluna o ka pakaukau* - We left the packages on the table.
> *Ke kau mai nei na ie laua'e maluna a'e o ka lanai* - The baskets of ferns are hanging above the porch.

Ilalo - below, down (denotes motion downward)

E iho aku ana lakou ilalo e kali ai ia kakou - They will go below to wait for us.

Iho aku nei makou ilalo iloko o ke ana - We went down into the cave.

Malalo - under

Ke pee maila oia malalo o ka hale - He is hiding under the house.

Imua - to the front (denotes motion forward)

E nee aku oukou imua - move to the front; move forward.

Mamua - before (expressing time), in front

Ua hiki makou i kauhale mamua o ka hola ekolu - We arrived home before three o'clock.

E hoʻea aku ana lakou mamua o makou - They will arrive before us.

Ku mai ana lakou mamua o makou - They stood in front of us.

Ihope - to the back (denotes motion backward)

E nee aku oukou apau ihope - All of you, move to the back.

Mahope - after (expressing time), behind (expressing place)

E hele aku ana makou mahope o ko lakou hoʻi ana mai - We will go out after they come home.

Aia ko lakou hale mahope o ka hale kuai - Their house is behind the store.

Iloko - in, into (denotes motion inward)

E waiho aku oe i kela mau noho iloko o kela lumi - Put those chairs in that room.

Ua holo aku nei ke kia iloko o ka ulu laau - The deer ran into the forest.

Maloko - in, inside, within

Ua waiho ke kaikamahine hana i ka lole maloko o ka lumi moe - The maid left the dress in the bedroom.

Noho makou maloko o ka lumi hookipa - We sat inside of the living room.

Aia ko makou aina maloko o ka aina nui o ka mahiko - Our property is within the large plantation land.

Iwaho - out (denotes motion outward)
Ua hele aku nei o Mele iwaho e nana i na mea kanu - Mary went out to look at the plants.

Mawaho - outside
Ku mai nei o Makaleka mawaho o ka puka - Margaret stood outside the door.

Iwaena - among, in the midst
Ua mahele makou i ke kala iwaena o makou - We divided the money among us.
Ku mai ana oia iwaena o kela po'e apau - He stood in the midst of all those people.

Mawaena - between
Ua mahele maua i ke kala mawaena o maua - We divided the money between us.

Iwaena konu - in the middle
E noho mai ana oia iwaena konu o ke alanui - He was sitting in the middle of the road.

Mawaena konu - in the center
Ua kukulu lakou i hale halawai mawaena konu o ka paka - They built a meeting house in the center of the park.

Maha'i - beside, next to
Ku ihola oia maha'i o'u i ka halawai - He stood beside me at the meeting.
E kukulu aku ana oia i kona home maha'i o ko'u home - He will build his home next to mine.

Vocabulary

ka ua - the rain
ka ume - the drawer
haalele - to leave a place

hiki - to arrive
  hiki aku - arrive there
  hiki mai - arrive here

ka hola - the hour
kauhale - home where one lives
ke kia - the deer
ke kii hoomana'o - the statue, the monument
ku - to stand
ka lumi - the room
ka lumi aina - the dining room
ka lumi hookipa - the living room

ka lumi kuke - the kitchen
ka lumi moe - the bedroom
ka paka - the park
ka pakaukau - the desk, the table
Poaha - Thursday
poha - to shine, as the sun; to burst, as a bubble
waiho - to leave something; to place

Exercise

Read and translate into English

1. E komo mai iloko o ka hale. 2. Ua hele mai nei lakou mahope iho o ka hola eono. 3. E kali mai oukou ia'u a hiki aku au. 4. Ua noho makou i kauhale a pau ka ua. 5. Ke noho maila ka ilio maha'i o ke keiki. 6. Mai hele mai oe a hike i ka Poaha. 7. Ke poha mai nei ka la mahope o ka ua. 8. Ke noho maila lakou maloko o ka lumi hookipa. 9. Ua holo mai nei ke kia mai ka ulu laau mai. 10. Mai pani aku oe i ka puka o ka lumi kuke. 11. Ke ku nei ke kii hoomana'o nui iwaena konu o ka paka. 12. E kii aku oe i ka peni maloko o ka ume o ka pakaukau.

Translate into Hawaiian

1. Do not close the door of the living room. 2. The large monument stands in the center of the park. 3. Go and get my pencil in the drawer of my desk. 4. They came after six o'clock. 5. Do not come into the house. 6. Let us wait for them until they get here. 7. The dog sits beside the boy. 8. We stayed at home until the rain stopped. 9. The sun shone after the rain. 10. They are sitting in the kitchen. 11. Do not go until Thursday. 12. The deer ran from the forest.

HAAWINA IWAKALUAKUMAMAHIKU
(Lesson Twenty-seven)

CONJUNCTIONS

Conjunctions are link words. They connect words, groups of words, sentences or parts of sentences.

A, ame - and

A connects compound sentences.
> *Mehana ka la a ke ulu nei na mea kanu* - The sun is warm and the plants are growing.

It connects compound predicates.
> *Ke himeni nei kamalii a ke hulahula nei* - The children are singing and dancing.

It also connects two objects preceded by an indefinite article.
> *Ua ako aku nei oia i loke a i kiele* - She picked a rose and a gardenia.

Ame connects compound subjects.
> *Ke heluhelu nei o Keoki ame Me i ka mea hou* - George and May are reading the news.

It also connects two objects preceded by the definite article.
> *Ua ako aku nei oia i ka loke ame ke kiele* - She picked the rose and the gardenia.

A - until

Ua noho makou me ia a pau ka hana - We stayed with her until the work was done.

A ... paha - or

Ka nui o keia aina he elua eka, oi aku a emi mai paha - The area of this land is two acres, more or less.

Note: *Paha* is an expression of doubt (believe, or maybe, perhaps). *Ua hele aku nei paha lakou i kahakai* - I believe they went to the beach.

Aka - but

Omamalu ka la aka aohe ua mai - The day is cloudy but it does not rain.

Ina - if

E kali aku ana au ia oe ina oe e hele koke mai - I shall wait for you if you come quickly.

No ka mea - because

Ua kali iho nei au ia oe no ka mea ua hele koke mai ne oe - I waited for you because you came quickly.

Oiai - while

E a'o pono oe ia lakou oiai lakou he opiopio - Teach them properly while they are young.

Vocabulary

ka i'a - the fish
ka ha'i'olele - the speech
hoomakaukau - to prepare, to make ready
kaula'i - to dry
ke kiaaina - the governor
koho - to vote

ka la - the day, the sun
makaukau - to be ready
ka malihini - the guest, the stranger
ka meia - the mayor
ka pelekikena - the president
ka puuku - the treasurer

Exercise

Read and translate into English

1. Ua hele aku nei o Kale ame Maliana i ke kula. 2. E hoʻihoʻi aku ana na keiki kane i na papale ame na kuka. 3. Ke hoomakaukau mai nei o Keoki i ka haʻiʻolelo a e heluhelu mai ana ia kakou. 4. E koho aku ana kakou i pelekikena a i puuku. 5. Ua makaukau ka mea ai aka e kali aku ana kakou a hiki mai ka poʻe malihini. 6. Ke hoʻi mai nei na kaikamahine no ka mea ua ike mai nei lakou ia kakou. 7. E kii aku ana o Hanale ia oukou ina oukou e kahea mai iaia. 8. E kaulaʻi kakou i ka iʻa oiai ka la iluna. 9. E noho ana makou maloko o ka hale pule a kii mai oe ia makou. 10. E koho aku ana oe i meia a i kiaaina paha.

Translate into Hawaiian

1. John went to get you because you called him. 2. We voted for a president and a treasurer. 3. Henry and Margaret went to school. 4. You will run for mayor or for governor. 5. George will write the speech and will read it to us. 6. The food is ready but we will wait until the guests arrive. 7. We sat in the church until he came to get us. 8. The boys are returning the hats and the coats. 9. Let us dry the fish while the sun is up. 10. The girls will come home if they see us.

Review

Read and translate into English

1. Ua hele na poʻe apau i ka pule i ka La Pule nei. 2. Ua ike lakou i na hoaaloha. 3. Ua himeni lakou i na mele o ka hale pule. 4. Ke pau ka pule, e hoʻi mai ana na poʻe apau i kauhale. 5. Ua hele mai nei na hoaaloha e ike ia lakou. 6. Noho na hoaaloha e ai. 7. Ke paani nei na keiki. 8. E kali ana lakou a makaukau ka mea ai. 9. Paani na keiki a hoomakaukau na makua i ka mea ai. 10. Ua ai lakou apau iloko o ka lumi aina nui. 11. Ua hoʻi na hoaaloha, ua pau ka ai ana.

Translate into Hawaiian

1. The children went to school. 2. They read stories in school. 3. The teacher taught them to read. 4. The parents stayed at home to do the work. 5. The children play in school and they learn their lessons. 6. The parents wait for the children to come home from school. 7. Our friends came to see us. 8. We invited them to stay to eat. 9. They left after they ate. 10. We all prayed before eating.

HAAWINA IWAKALUAKUMAMAWALU
(Lesson Twenty-eight)

THE PASSIVE VOICE

The passive voice is formed by adding *ia* to the verb.
Conjugation of the Passive Voice

PRESENT TENSE

Singular

ke kahea ia mai nei au - I am being called
ke kahea ia mai nei oe - you are being called
ke kahea ia mai nei oia - he/she is being called
ke kahea ia mai nei oiala - he/she (over there) is being called
ke kahea ia mai nei oinei - he/she (over here) is being called

Dual (Two)

ke kahea ia mai nei kaua - we (you and I) are being called
ke kahea ia mai nei maua -we (he/she and I) are being called
ke kahea ia mai nei olua - you (two) are being called

ke kahea ia mai nei laua - they (two) are being called
ke kahea ia mai nei laua ala - they (two over there) are being called
ke kahea ia mai nei laua nei - they (two over here) are being called

Plural (More than two)

ke kahea ia mai nei kakou - we (you, they and I) are being called
ke kahea ia mai nei makou - we (they and I) are being called
ke kahea ia mai nei oukou - you (more than two) are being called
ke kahea ia mai nei lakou - they (more than two) are being called
ke kahea ia mai nei lakou ala - they (more than two over there) are
  being called
ke kahea ia mai nei lakou nei - they (more than two over here) are
  being called

PAST TENSE

Singular

ua kahea ia mai nei au - I was called
ua kahea ia mai nei oe - you were called
ua kahea ia mai nei oia - he/she was called
ua kahea ia mai nei oiala - he/she (over there) was called
ua kahea ia mai nei oinei - he/she (over here) was called

Dual (Two)

ua kahea ia mai nei kaua - we (you and I) were called
ua kahea ia mai nei maua - we (he/she and I) were called
ua kahea ia mai nei olua - you (two) were called
ua kahea ia mai nei laua - they (two) were called
ua kahea ia mai nei laua ala - they (two over there) were called
ua kahea ia mai nei laua nei - they (two over here) were called

Plural (More than two)

ua kahea ia mai nei kakou - we (you, they and I) were called
ua kahea ia mai nei makou - we (they and I) were called
ua kahea ia mai nei oukou - you (more than two) were called
ua kahea ia mai nei lakou - they (more than two) were called
ua kahea ia mai nei lakou ala - they (more than two over there)
were called
ua kahea ia mai nei lakou nei - they (more than two over here) were
called

FUTURE TENSE

Singular

e kahea ia mai ana au - I will be called
e kahea ia aku ana oe - you will be called
e kahea ia aku ana oia - he/she will be called
e kahea ia aku ana oiala - he/she (over there) will be called
e kahea ia mai ana oinei - he/she (over here) will be called

Dual (Two)

e kahea ia mai ana kaua - we (you and I) will be called
e kahea ia mai ana maua - we (he/she and I) will be called
e kahea ia aku ana olua - you (two) will be called
e kahea ia aku ana laua - they (two) will be called
e kahea ia aku ana laua ala - they (two over there) will be called
e kahea ia mai ana laua nei - they (two over here) will be called

Plural (More than two)

e kahea ia mai ana kakou - we (you, they and I) will be called
e kahea ia mai ana makou - we (they and I) will be called

e kahea ia aku ana oukou - you (more than two) will be called
e kahea ia aku ana lakou - they (more than two) will be called
e kahea ia aku ana lakou ala - they (more than two over there) will
      be called
e kahea ia mai ana lakou nei - they (more than two over here) will
      be called

    Some Hawaiian verbs denote a state of being, as *naha* - to be broken; *eha* - to be hurt; *loaa* - to be found, received, etc. These verbs include the verb to be and do not require the suffix *ia* for the passive voice. The preposition "by" is expressed by *i* or *ia*.

    Examples:

Ua naha ke kiaha i ke kaikamahine - the glass was broken by the
      girl
Ua eha keia kaikamahine ia oe - this girl was hurt by you
Ua loaa ke kala ia Moke - the money was found by Moses; the
      money was received by Moses

    A Hawaiian sentence in the past tense may be translated in the present tense.

    Examples:

Ua naha ke kiaha - the glass is broken
Ua eha keia kaikamahine - this girl is hurt
Ua loaa ke kala - the money is found; the money is received

    However, the verb *wawahi* means "to break" and when we say *ke wawahi ia nei ke kiaha* we mean "the glass is now being broken."

    The passive voice is used more frequently than in English although Hawaiian sentences in the passive voice are often translated in the active voice.

Vocabulary

aihue - to steal

eha - to be hurt

i - by

i ka la apopo - tomorrow

i ka po nei - last night

i keia manawa - now

i nehinei - yesterday

ia - by

iole lapaki - rabbit

uala - potato

upa - scissors

ho'iliili - to save, to accumulate

ka - to make a net

kaa - to roll, as a stone

kanaka lawai'a - fisherman

kanaka mahi'ai - farmer

kanaka poa - robber

kanu - to plant

ki - to shoot

lohe - to hear

mahi'ai - to cultivate

maka'ika'i - to go sightseeing

mea oia'i'o - truth

mokulele - airplane

naloale - to be lost

po - night

po'e maka'ika'i - visitors, tourists, people who go sightseeing

Exercise

Read and translate into English

1. Ua ike ia ka mokulele e na po'e maka'ika'i i nehinei. 2. Ua ki ia ka iole lapaki e ke keiki kolohe. 3. Ua aihue ia ke kala e ke kanaka poa i ka po nei. 4. E lohe ia ana ka mea hou e na po'e apau i ka la apopo. 5. Ke ha'i ia mai nei ka mea oia'i'o ia kakou i keia manawa. 6. E kukulu ia aku ana kela hale e keia po'e kanaka. 7. E ho'iliili ia aku ana ke kala e na po'e maka'ika'i. 8. Ke kuai ia nei keia aina e makou i ke aupuni. 9. Ua mahiai ia keia aina e ke kanaka

mahi'ai. 10. Ke ka ia nei ka upena e ke kanaka lawai'a. 11. E eha ana kakou i keia pohaku. 12. Ua naloale ka upa ia oe.

Translate into Hawaiian

1. That house will be built by those men. 2. That money is being saved by the visitors. 3. This land was given to them by the governor. 4. This land will be cultivated by the farmer. 5. That net is being made by the fisherman. 6. The truth will be told to us now. 7. The news is being heard by everyone. 8. The money was stolen by the robber last night. 9. This airplane will be seen by the tourists tomorrow. 10. The rabbit was shot by the naughty boy yesterday. 11. We were hurt by the large rock. 12. The scissors were lost by Mary.

NUMERICAL DITTY

Kahi, kahi, kahi olona - (*kahi* also means to scrape or shave) shave, shave, scrape the olona bark

Lua, lua, lua wai - (*lua* also means hole) a hole, a hole, a water hole

Kolu, kolu, kula kaimana - *kolu* means column, *kula* means gold and *kaimana* means diamond

Ha, ha ha opae - (*ha* means to feel) feel, feel, feel for the opae

Lima, lima, lima kokua - (*lima* also means hand) a helping hand

Ono, ono, ono mea ono - (*ono* means tasty or sweet) cake is sweet

Hiku, hiku, hiku kialo - *hiku* is a hook to catch hold of things

Walu, walu, walu popoki - *walu* is the scratch of a cat

Iwa, iwa, iwa kiani - *kiani* is to wave gently as a small flag

Umi, umi, umiumi kao - *umiumi* is a beard like that of a goat

HAAWINA IWAKALUAKUMAMAIWA
(Lesson Twenty-nine)

NUMERALS
Cardinal Numbers

The fundamental or basic Hawaiian numbers are:

kahi - one	**ono** - six
lua - two	**hiku** - seven
kolu - three	**walu** - eight
ha - four	**iwa** - nine
lima - five	**umi** - ten

ole and **he ole** both mean zero.

The basic numbers *lua, kolu,* etc. require the prefix *e* to form the cardinal numbers. *Kahi,* however, requires *hoo* to indicate quantity and *e* to designate time, page, chapter, lesson, etc.

Examples:

hookahi penikala - one pencil   *mokuna ekahi* - chapter one
hola ekahi - one o'clock   *haawina ekahi* - lesson one
ao'ao ekahi - page one

The cardinal numbers one to ten are:

ekahi - one	**eono** - six
elua - two	**ehiku** - seven
ekolu - three	**ewalu** - eight
eha - four	**eiwa** - nine
elima - five	**umi** - ten

Numbers eleven (ten and one) to nineteen (ten and nine) are formed by prefixing *umikumama* to the basic numbers.

umikumamakahi - eleven
umikumamalua - twelve
umikumamakolu - thirteen
umikumamaha - fourteen
umikumamalima - fifteen
umikumamaono - sixteen
umikumamahiku - seventeen
umikumamawalu - eighteen
umikumamaiwa - nineteen
Iwakalua is twenty.

Numbers twenty-one (twenty and one) to twenty-nine (twenty and nine) are formed by prefixing *iwakaluakumama* to the basic numbers.

iwakaluakumamakahi - twenty-one
iwakaluakumamalua - twenty-two
iwakaluakumamakolu - twenty-three
iwakaluakumamaha - twenty-four
iwakaluakumamalima - twenty-five
iwakaluakumamaono - twenty-six
iwakaluakumamahiku - twenty-seven
iwakaluakumamawalu - twenty-eight
iwakaluakumamaiwa - twenty-nine

The second *ma* in *kumama* is often dropped, as *umikumakahi* for eleven, *iwakaluakumalua* for twenty-two, etc.

Numbers thirty, forty, fifty, sixty, seventy, eighty and ninety are formed by prefixing *kana* to the basic numbers *kolu, ha, lima, ono, hiku, walu* and *iwa*.

kanakolu - thirty   **kanahiku** - seventy
kanaha - forty   **kanawalu** - eighty
kanalima - fifty   **kanaiwa** - ninety
kanaono - sixty

The *w* in *walu* of numbers eighteen, twenty-eight, thirty-eight, etc. may be omitted and the second *a* in *kumama* changed to *o* for euphony, as *umikumamoalu* for eighteen; *iwakaluakumamoalu* for twenty-eight; *kanakolukumamoalu* for thirty-eight, etc. However, this usage is uncommon.

The English numbers "hundred," "thousand" and "million" have been Hawaiianized to *haneli, kaukani* and *miliona*.

"One hundred and one," etc. is expressed by *hookahi haneli me ekahi*, etc.

Examples:
haneli - hundred
hookahi haneli - one hundred
hookahi haneli me ekahi - one hundred and one
kaukani - thousand
hookahi kaukani - one thousand
hookahi kaukani me ekahi - one thousand and one
miliona - million
hookahi miliona - one million
hookahi miliona me ekahi - one million and one

When a numeral is the object of a verb, *i* must be placed immediately before the number, as *ua lawe aku nei ke kaikamahine i elua peni* - the girl took two pens.

Numerals generally precede the nouns they modify.

Exercise

Read and translate into English

1. Ua aku mai nei kela kanaka i elima kala ia oe. 2. E haawi mai oe ia'u i hookahi kii. 3. Ke lawe mai nei ke kaikamahine i elua apala ia kaua. 4. E helu aku ana au i umikumamakahi peni. 5. Ua heluhelu mai nei ke kaikamahine i ka mokuna ekahi o ka moolelo. 6. E lawe aku oe i elua mea ono ia laua. 7. Ke kukulu nei oia i ekolu hale hou. 8. E kakau aku ana o Mele i ekolu leka. 9. Ua ai makou i ka hola umikumamalua. 10. E holo aku ana ka moku i ka hola eono.

Translate into Hawaiian

1. The man will read chapter seven to them. 2. The boat sailed at eight o'clock. 3. She is returning twelve pens to the school. 4. We will eat at one o'clock. 5. They counted nine apples. 6. Those men are building five new houses. 7. Give me ten oranges. 8. Margaret wrote six letters. 9. Take two cakes to them. 10. This woman will pay me eleven dollars.

HAAWINA KANAKOLU
(Lesson Thirty)

NUMERALS
Ordinal Numbers

ka mua - first

ka lua - second

ke kolu - third

ka ha - fourth

ka lima - fifth

ke ono - sixth

ka hiku - seventh

ka walu - eighth

ka iwa - ninth

ka umi - tenth

ka umikumamahaki - eleventh

ka umikumamalua - twelfth

ka umikumamaiwa - nineteenth

ka iwakalua - twentieth

ke kanakolu - thirtieth

ke kanaha - fortieth

ke kanalima - fiftieth

ka haneli - hundredth

ke kaukani - thousandth

ka miliona - millionth

The ordinal numbers, with the exception of *ka mua* (first) are formed by placing the definite article *ka* before the basic numbers.

Fractions

Fractions are designated by the word *hapa,* meaning fragment or part. *Hapa,* however, is also the Hawaiianized word for "half," as *hookahi me ka hapa* - one and a half.

Hawaiian for "five cents" is *hapaumi* (half of ten). *Kenikeni* is the Hawaiianized word for ten cents.

The numerators of fractions are expressed by cardinal numbers and the denominator by the basic numbers (Lesson 16) preceded by *hapa*.

Examples:
hapalua - half
hookahi hapalua - one-half
hapakolu - third
elua hapakolu - two thirds
hapaha - fourth
ekolu hapaha - three-fourths
hapawalu - eighth
elima hapawalu - five-eighths
hapaumi - tenth
eiwa hapaumi - nine-tenths
hookahi hapa haneli - one-hundredth
elua hapa haneli - two-hundredths
eha hapa kaukani - four-thousandths

In ancient times the Hawaiians counted by fours. Their system was as follows:

Four was called *kauna*.

Forty was called *kaau*.

Four hundred was called *lau*.

Four thousand was called *mano*.

Forty thousand was called *kini*.

Four hundred thousand was called *lehu*.

Lehu was their highest number. To express abundance without limit, a Hawaiian would say, *Hele a mano a kini a lehu*, meaning the number exceeded *mano*, *kini*, and even *lehu*.

Exercise

Read and translate into English

1. Ua noho makou iloko o ka lumi nui no ekolu hapaha hola.

2. O ka ha keia o ka haawina iloko o keia puke. 3. Ke heluhelu nei

na haumana i ka lima o ka haawina i keia manawa. 4. Ua ai na kanaka hana i ka hapalua o ka mea ono i nehinei. 5. Ua olelo mai nei ke kumukula i na haumana e ha'i aku i ka walu o ka haawina. 6. E kali aku ana makou iaia a hiki i ke ono o ka la. 7. E holo aku ana na keikikane no hookahi hapaha mile i ka la apopo. 8. Ke hanai nei na keiki nui i na ilio i hookahi hapa kolu o ka mea ai. 9. O ka la mua keia o ke kula. 10. Ua ai na keiki liilii i hookahi apala me ka hapa.

Translate into Hawaiian

1. The teacher told the pupils to recite the eighth lesson. 2. We sat in the large room for three-fourths of an hour. 3. This is the fourth lesson in the book. 4. We will wait for her until the sixth day. 5. The workingmen ate half of the cake. 6. The pupils read the fifth lesson of the book yesterday. 7. The boys will run one-fourth of a mile tomorrow. 8. Those boys are feeding the dogs one-third of the food. 9. This is the first day at school. 10. This boy ate one apple and a half.

HAAWINA KANAKOLUKUMAMAKAHI
(Lesson Thirty-one)

NAMES OF DAYS AND MONTHS

The words *i kela* precede "week" *(pule)*, "month" *(mahina)* and "year" *(makahiki)*, while *aku nei* follow them to express "last week" *(i kela pule aku nei)*, "last month" *(i kela mahina aku nei)*, and "last year" *(i kela makahiki aku nei)*.

The words *i keia* precede "week," "month" and "year," while *aʻe* follows them to express "next week" *(i keia pule aʻe)*, "next month" *(i keia mahina aʻe)* and "next year" *(i keia makahiki aʻe)*.

I nehinei expresses "yesterday," *i keia la* expresses "today" and *i ka la apopo* expresses "tomorrow."

Vocabulary

Poʻakahi - Monday	**pule** - week
Poʻalua - Tuesday	**Ianuali** - January
Poʻakolu - Wednesday	**Pepeluali** - February
Poʻaha - Thursday	**Malaki** - March
Poʻalima - Friday	**Apelila** - April
Poʻaono - Saturday	**Mei** - May
La pule - Sunday	**Iune** - June
kekona - second	**Iulae** - July
minuke - minute	**Aukake** - August
hola - hour	**Kemakemapa** - September
la - day	**Okakopa** - October

Nowemapa - November   **la nui** - holiday
Kekemapa - December   **po** - night
mahina - month   **i ka po nei** - last night
makahiki - year   **i keia po** - tonight
la hanau - birthday   **i ka po apopo** - tomorrow night

Hawaiian Seasons

Ke kupulau - spring   **Ka ha'ule lau** - autumn
Ke kau - summer   **Ka hooilo** - winter

Examples:

Ka la hea keia o ka mahina? - What day of the month is this?
Ka la umikumamakahi keia o Iune. - This is the eleventh day of June.
Apopo ana ka la umikumamalua. - Tomorrow will be the twelfth day.
Ka la umi o Iune o nehinei. - Yesterday was the tenth of June.
Ho'i mai oia i ka la ekolu o Malaki. - He came home on the third day of March.
I kela pule aku nei - last week
Hookahi pule mai keia la aku - one week from today
Hookahi pule mai ka poakahi aku - one week from Monday
Ka mahina hea? - What month?
Ka mahina o Kekemapa. - The month of December

Exercise

Read and translate into English

1. Ka puke hea kau i lawe ai? 2. Heaha ka inoa o ka puke au i lawe mai nei? 3. Owai kou inoa? 4. Owai ka inoa o kou makuahine? 5. Ehia alani o loko o ke pola? 6. Na wai keia penikala? 7. Ehia ou makahiki? 8. Ka wai peni keia? 9. Ka peni hea? 10. Kela mau peni ma ka papahele. 11. Na keia keiki kela mau peni. 12. Heaha keia? 13. He kii kena. 14. He aha ka haawina o keia la? 15. Aole i

maopopo iaʻu. 16. E hoʻi ana au. 17. No ke aha mai? 18. He nui ka hana o kauhale.

Translate into Hawaiian

1. What is the lesson for today? 2. I do not know. 3. What is your name? 4. What is your father's name? 5. What is that? 6. This is a picture. 7. How many apples are in the bowl? 8. I am going home. 9. Why? 10. There is much to do at home. 11. How old are you? 12. I am nineteen years old. 13. Whose books are these? 14. Which books? 15. Those books on the table. 16. They are mine.

View of the church and some houses in Kaunakakai taken from the pier.

HAAWINA KANAKOLUKUMAMALUA
(Lesson Thirty-two)

INTERROGATIVES

Wai, Who? *Aha,* what? and *hea,* where? are the stems of Hawaiian interrogatives. The interrogative pronouns are *ehia?* how many? *ia wai?* to whom? *ihea?* where? *owai?* who? who is? who are? *heaha?* what? what is? what are? *ka mea hea?* which? which one? which thing? *ka wai? ko wai? na wai? no wai?* whose? *no ke aha?* what for? why?

Examples:

Ehia haumana o kau papa? How many pupils in your class? or how many pupils do you have in your class?

Ia wai kakou e hele aku ai? To whom shall we go?

Owai o oukou ka mea kala? Which one of you has money?

Owai keia kaikamahine? Who is this girl?

Ka mea hea kau i* lawe ai? Which one did you take?

Ko wai kuka kena? Whose coat is that?

No ke aha oe i hele mai nei? Why did you come?

E hele ana o Keoki ihea? Where is George going?

In asking a person's name, a Hawaiian always says, "owai kou inoa," literally translated, "*who* is your name?" Never "heaha kou inoa," what is your name? Also a Hawaiian never asks, "Owai oe?" who are you? This is an insulting question. It implies "Who do you think you are?"

---

* *i* before a verb denotes past tense.

Vocabulary

aha - stem of the interrogative "what?"

ehia - how many? how old? as ehia ou makahiki? how old are you?

ia wai - to whom?

ihea - where? to what place?

i kauhale - at home

owai - who? who is? who are? what? when asking a person's name, as: owai kou inoa? what is your name?

hana - work; to work
   ka hana - work; the work

he nui ka - plenty of; lots of

hea - stem of the interrogative where? which?

heaha - what? what is? what are?

ka mea hea - which? which one? which thing?

ka wai - whose?

ko wai - whose?

na wai - whose? belongs to whom?

no keaha - what for? why?

no wai - whose? belongs to whom?

wai - stem of the interrogative who?

Exercise

Read and translate into English

1. Ka la iwakalua kumamakolu o Ianuali ka la hanau o ko'u makuahine.   2. Ka la umikumamakolu o Okakopa, makahiki umikumamawalu haneli me kanawalu kumakahi. 3. E ha'i mai i na mahina. 4. Ka la pule ka la hope o ka pule. He la hoomaha ia. 5. Poakahi ka la mua o ka pule. 6. Ehiku la o ka pule. 7. Kanakolu la o ka mahina. 8. He la nui ka la umikumakahi o Iune. 9. Ka la hanau ia o ke Alii Kamehameha Ekahi. 10. Ka la umi o Iune ka la hanau o Ko'u makuakane.

Translate into Hawaiian

1. The 14th of July, 1977. 2. January 23rd is my mother's birthday 3. June 11th is a holiday. 4. It is the birthday of King Kamehameha First. 5. Name the months in the year. 6. Name the days of the week. 7. Monday is the first day of the week. 8. There are seven days in the week. 9. There are thirty days in the month. 10. August thirty-first is my brother's birthday.   11. This is Thursday. 12. June 10th is the birthday of my father.

HAAWINA KANAKOLUKUMAMAKOLU
(Lesson Thirty-three)

TIME OF DAY

The following are ways of expressing the time of day:

Hola ehia keia? - What time is it?

Hola ekahi keia - It is one o'clock.

Hapalua hola eha keia - It is half past four.

Hapaha i hala o ka hola ekolu - It is a quarter past three o'clock.

Umi minuke i hala o ka hola eono - It is ten minutes past six.

Iwakalua minuke i hala o ka hola ewalu - It is twenty minutes past eight.

Umikumamalima minuke i koe kani ka hola eiwa - It is fifteen minutes to nine.

Elima minuke i koe kani ka hola elua - It is five minutes to two.

Hola umikumamalua o ke awakea - It is twelve o'clock noon.

Hola umikumamalua o ke aumoe - It is twelve o'clock midnight.

Hola ehia hoʻi, aole i maopopo iaʻu ka manawa - I don't know the time.

I ka hola ehia? - At what time?

I ka hola ehiku o ke ahiahi - At seven o'clock in the evening.

Ma kahi paha o ka hola eiwa - At about nine o'clock.

As in English, the minutes after the hour are expressed by *i hala* - past. However, the minutes before the hour are expressed by *i koe* - remaining.

O'clock is often omitted in English, but *hola* is never omitted in Hawaiian.

Example:

I ka hola ehia lakou i hoʻea mai ai? At what time did they arrive?

Ma kahi paha o ka hola ekolu. At about three o'clock.

E hiki aku ana makou i ka la apopo - we (they and I) shall arrive, (there) tomorrow.

E hiki mai ana lakou i keia la - They will arrive (here) today.

E hoʻi aku ana o Mele ma i keia ahiahi - Mary and the others will go home this evening. Mary and the others will go back this evening. Mary and the others will return (there) this evening.

Poʻahia lakou i hele ai? What day did they (more than two) go?

Poʻahia lakou i hoʻea mai ai? What day did they (more than two) arrive (here)?

E hoʻi mai ana o Keoni i keia po - John will come home tonight. John will come back tonight. John will return (here) tonight.

Vocabulary

mamua - before

mahope - after

Lakou i hele ai? - Did they (more than two) go?

haalele - left

ke kaa ahi - the train

kokoke - almost; near

Exercise

Read and translate into English

1. E hiki aku ana makou i kauhale mamua o ka hola umikumamalua o ke awakea. 2. Hola ehia keia? 3. Hapaha i koe kani ka hola elua. 4. Elima minuke i koe kani ka hola ekolu. 5. Iwakalua minuke i hala o ka hola eha. 6. I ka hola ehia lakou i hele ai? 7. Haalele lakou i kauhale i ka hapaha i hala o ka hola umikumamakahi. 8. E haalele ana ke kaa ahi i ka hola elua. 9. Hoʻi mai lakou i ka hola umikumamalua o ke aumoe. 10. Kokoke kani ka hola eiwa.

Translate into Hawaiian

    1. At what time did they leave? 2. They left home at three o'clock.   3. We shall arrive home before two o'clock in the afternoon. 4. The train will leave at four o'clock. 5. What time is it? 6. It is a quarter to four. 7. It is five minutes to one. 8. It is midnight. 9. It is almost ten. 10. At what time did they go?

A service station in Kaunakakai.

HAAWINA KANAKOLUKUMAMAHA
(Lesson Thirty-four)

PERSONAL PRONOUNS
Possessive Case (Third Group)

The third group of possessive pronouns is a combination of the simple preposition *na* or *no* (for) and the personal pronoun in the nominative case (Lesson one).

The *a* of the pronoun *au*, first person singular, is dropped and *na* or *no* is used in its place. The word then becomes *naʻu* or *noʻu*.

The pronoun *oe*, second person singular (Lesson two) is dropped and the words *au* or *ou* are used in its place. The word then becomes *nau* or *nou*.

The pronoun *oia*, third person, singular, is dropped and the word *na* or *no* is used in its place; thus the words become *nana* or *nona*. However, with the particle *ala* or *nei*, the pronoun *ia* third person singular is used. But the *a* is dropped and the letter *i* is joined to the particle for the sake of euphony, and the words become *naiala, nainei, noiala, noinei*.

Examples:
Singular

naʻu; noʻu - Belongs to me; for me; mine
nau; nou - Belongs to you; for you, yours
nana; nona - Belongs to her/him; for her/him; hers; his
na iala; no iala - Belongs to her/him (over there); for her/him (over there); hers/his (over there)
nainei; noinei - Belongs to her/him (over here); for her/him (over here); his (over here); hers (over here)

Dual (two)

na kaua; no kaua - Belongs to us (you and me); for us (you and me); our (your and my)

na maua; no maua - Belongs to us (him/her and me); For us (him/her and me); Ours (hers/his and mine)

na olua; no olua - Belongs to you (two); for you (two); yours (two)

na laua; no laua - Belongs to them (two); for them (two); theirs (two)

na laua ala; no laua ala - Belongs to them (two over there); for them (two over there); theirs (two over there)

na laua nei; no laua nei - Belongs to them (two over here); for them (two over here); theirs (two over here)

Plural (More than two)

na kakou; no kakou - Belongs to us / For us (you them and me); Ours (your their and my)

na makou; no makou - Belongs to us / for us (them and me); Ours (theirs and my)

na oukou; no oukou - Belongs to you / for you (more than two); Yours (more than two)

na lakou; no lakou - Belongs to them/ for them (more than two); Theirs (more than two)

na lakou ala; no lakou ala - Belongs to them/ for them (more than two over there); Theirs (more than two over there)

na lakou nei; no lakou nei - Belongs to them/ for them (more than two over here); Theirs (more than two over here)

Vocabulary

ke kula nui o Hawaii - University of Hawaii

nui na keiki - many children

Exercise

Read and translate into English

1. Na ko'u kaikunane keia mau keiki. 2. Nona keia home. 3. Na ka'u keiki keia puke. 4. He puke a'o olelo keia. 5. Ua kuai oia mai ka hale ku'ai mai. 6. He puke maikai, he puke a'o olelo. 7. He keiki akamai oia. 8. Ke hele nei oia i ke kula nui o Hawaii. 9. Makemake oia e lilo i kumukula. 10. Nui na keiki e hele nei i ke kula nui o Hawaii.

Translate into Hawaiian

1. My son goes to the University of Hawaii. 2. His sister is a teacher. 3. Those are my sister's children. 4. My son wishes to be a teacher. 5. My daughter bought that book from the book store. 6. It is a good book, it is an English grammar. 7. My son's name is George and his sister's name is Elizabeth. 8. She is married and has two children, a boy and a girl. 9. The boy's name is John and his sister's name is Mary. 10. Her husband's name is Henry.

VOCABULARY

Hawaiian - English

a - and

a - of; to; until

a - to be burning, as a fire or lamp

a iala - her/his (over there), of her/of him (over there)

a ianei (or **a inei**) - her/his (over here), of her/ of him (over here)

a oukou - your/ of you (more than two)

a olua - your/ of you (two)

a kaua - our (your and my), of us (you and me)

a kakou - our (your, their and my), of us (you, them and me)

a laua - their/ of them (two)

a laua ala - their/ of them (two over there)

a laua nei - their/ of them (two over here)

a lakou - their/ of them (more than two)

a lakou ala - their/ of them (more than two over there)

a lakou nei - their/ of them (more than two over here)

a maua - our/ of us (her/his and my) (her/him and me)

a makou - our/ of us (their/them and my/me)

a . . . paha - or

ae - to agree; to consent; to permit

ae aku - to agree with him; to consent to him; to permit him

ae mai - to agree with me; to consent to me; to permit me

ae - yes

ae, ke aloha no! - yes, greetings! (answer or response to a greeting)

a'e - a directive - motion upward or sideways

ai - to eat

aihue - to steal

a'o - to learn

a'o - to teach

a'o aku - to teach them

a'o mai - to teach us; to teach me

aoao - page; side

a'ohe - does not have; has not; have not

a'ohe a'u (or **a'ohe o'u**) - I do not have; I have no _____

a'ole - no; not

au - I

au - your; of you

a'u - my; of me

Aukake - August

aumoe - late at night; midnight

auwe! - Oh! oh dear!

aha - stem of *heaha*

ahi - a kind of fish

ahi - fire; match

aka - but

akaaka - to be clear; to be distinct; to be plain

aka'aka - to laugh

akea - wide; broad; large; roomy

aku - a fish

aku - a directive - motion away from speaker

ala - article of location meaning there, over there, in that direction

ala - fragrant; fragrance

ala - to be awake

ala - path; road; street; trail

ala hele - path; trail

alani - orange

alanui - road; street

aloha - love

aloha! - greeting; how do you do!

aloha, ea! - greetings! how do you do

alu - to be slack, as a rope or wire

ame - and; and with

Ameli'ka - America; American

ana - the "ing" ending

ana - the progressive form of a verb

ana - tense suffix

ana - her/his; of her/ of him

Ana - Anna; Ann

Ane - Annie

anei - an interogative word

apala - apple

Apelila - April

apono - to be approved; to be accepted; to be justified.
  e apono - to approve; to accept; to justify

awakea - noon

e - sign of the present or future tense

e - to; by

eiwa - nine

eiwa hapaumi - nine-tenths

eono - six

eono hapahiku - six-sevenths

eha' - four

eha' hapakaukani - four thousands

eha' hapalima - four fifths

e'ha - to be hurt; to be sore; to be in pain

ehia? - how many, how old?

ehiku - seven

ehiku hapawalu - seven-eighths

eka - acre

ekahi - one

ekalesia - religion (religious organization)

ekolu - three

ekolu hapaha - three-fourths

elemakule - old man

elema'kule - old men

Elena - Ellen

eleweka - elevator

Elikapeka - Elizabeth

elima - five

elima hapaono - five-sixths

elima minuke - five minutes
  elima minuke i hala o ka hola ekahi - five minutes past one
  elima minuke i koe kani ka hola umi - five minutes to ten

elua - two

elua hapahaneli - two hundredths

elua hapakolu - two thirds

emi - to be decreased in number or size; to be less; to be cheap

ewalu - eight

ewalu hapaiwa - eight ninths

i - objective sign before names of places

i - at, to, in, for, by

i - a, an

i - said

i akula - said to her/him/them

i ka la apopo - tomorrow

i ka po nei - last night

i kauhale - at home

i ke kula - to school, at school

i keia manawa - now, at this time

i maila - said (to me)

i mau - some

i nehinei - yesterday

i'a - fish

ia - at, to, by, for, about

ia - objective sign, before names of persons

ia - (ee-yah') Hawaiian pronunciation of the English word yard

ia - sign of the passive voice when used after a verb

ia oe - you, to you

ia oukou - you (more than two), to you (more than two)

ia olua - you (two), to you (two)

ia kaua - us (you and me), to us (you and me)

ia kakou - us, to us (you, him/her/ them and me)

ia laua - them (two), to them (two)

ia laua ala - them (two over there), to them (two over there)

ia laua nei - them (two over here), to them (two over here)

ia lakou - them (more than two), to them (more than two)

ia lakou ala - them (more than two over there), to them (more than two over there)

ia lakou nei - them (more than two over here), to them (more than two over here)

ia maua - us (her/him and me), to us (him/her and me)

ia makou - us (them and me), to us (them and me)

ia wai? - to whom?

iaia - her/him, to her/him

iaiala - her/him over there, to her/him over there

iaianei - her/him (over here), to her/him (over here)

ia'u - me, to me

Iakopa - Jacob

Ianuali - January

Iesu - Jesus

Ioane - John, Juan

Iokepa - Joseph

iole - mouse, rat

iole lapaki - rabbit

Iulae - July

Iune - June

ihea - where, where is/are, where to

Ihea aku nei oe? - Where have you been? Where did you go?

iho - self
    ia'u iho - myself
    ia oe iho - yourself

iho - to descend, to go down

ihope - backward

ike - to know, to perceive, to see
    e ike ia kaua - to see us

iki - a little bit, a little more, a little less

ilalo - below, down, downward

ili - to be vested in, to be derived, to be inherited, to fall or come to one, as an inheritance

iliili - an accumulation, a mass or heap; a large quantity, a pile; to be accumulated

iliili - little stones

ilio - dog

ilihune - poor

iloko - in, into

iluna - up, upward

imua - forward

ina' - if

inika - ink

inu - to drink

ipuhao - pot

ipukukui - lamp, light

ipupaka - smoking pipe

iwa - ninth

iwaena - in the midst, among

iwaena konu - in the middle

iwakalua - twenty

iwakaluakumaiwa - twenty-nine

iwakaluakumaono - twenty-six

iwakaluakumaha' - twenty-four

iwakaluakumahiku - twenty-seven

iwakaluakumakahi - twenty-one

iwakaluakumakolu - twenty-three

iwakaluakumalima - twenty-five

iwakaluakumalua - twenty-two

iwakaluakumamaiwa - twenty-nine

iwakaluakumamaono - twenty-six

iwakaluakumamaha - twenty-four

iwakaluakumamahiku - twenty-seven

iwakaluakumamakahi - twenty-one

iwakaluakumamakolu - twenty-three

iwakaluakumamalima - twenty-five

iwakaluakumamalua -twenty-two

iwakaluakumamawalu - twenty-eight

iwakaluakumamoalu - twenty-eight

iwakaluakumawalu - twenty-eight

o (emphatic) - an article used to point out the subject (before name of person)

o - of

o iala - he/she (over there), her/his (over there), of him/of her (over there)

o ianei (o inei) - he/she (over here), his/her (over there), of him/of her (over here)

o oukou - you/of you/your (more than two)

o olua - you/of you/your (two)

o kaua - our (your and my), of us (you and me), we (you and I)

o kakou - our (your, their and my), of us (you, them and ,me), we (you, they and I)

o laua - their/of them/they (two)

o laua ala - their/of them/they (two over there)

o laua nei - their/of them/they (two over here)

o lakou - their/of them/they (more than two)

o lakou ala - their/of them/they (more than two over there)

o lakou nei - their/of them/they (more than two over here)

o maua - our (his/her and my), of us (him/her and me), we (he/she and I)

o makou - our (their and my), of us (them and me), we (they and I)

oe - you

oi a'e - more

oi a'e ka maikai - better than

oia - to be true, to be correct

oia - he/she

oia - all right, O.K., okay

oiai - while

oiaio - truth, proof

oiala - he/she (over there)

oinei - he/she (over here)

o'u - my, of me

ou - your, of you

oukou - you (more than two)

ohelo - berry, strawberry

Okakopa - October

oki - to cut

ole - zero

olelo - language

olelo - to say; to speak; to tell something; to tell someone something

olelo aku - to say to him; to speak to him; to tell him

olelo mai - to say to me; to speak to me; to tell me

olua - you (two)

ona - Hawaiian pronunciation of the English word "owner"

ona - his/hers, of him/of her

ono - six, sixth

ono - tasty, sweet

opiopio - young

owai? - who? who is/who are?

owau - I

ua - sign of past tense

ua - rain

ua - to rain

uaki - watch

Uakinakona - Washington

uala - potato

uea - wire

u'i - pretty

u'i iki a'e - a little prettier

uiki - wick

Uilama - William

Uiliama - William

uuku - small, little

ume - drawer

umi - ten

umikumaiwa - nineteen

umikumaono - sixteen

umikumaha - fourteen

umikumahiku - seventeen

umikumakahi - eleven

umikumakolu - thirteen

umikumalima - fifteen

umikumalima minuke i hala o ka hola umi - fifteen minutes past ten

umikumamaiwa - nineteen

umikumamaono - sixteen

umikumamaha - fourteen

umikumamahiku - seventeen

umikumamakahi - eleven

umikumamakolu - thirteen

umikumamalima - fifteen

umikumamalua - twelve

umikumamawalu - eighteen

umikumamoalu - eighteen

umikumawalu - eighteen

uniona - union

upa' - scissors

ha - four, fourth

haalele - to leave a place

haawi - to give

haawi aku - to give away; to give to her/to him/to them (away from the speaker)

haawi mai - to give to me; to give this way (toward the speaker)

haawina - lesson

ha'i - to recite; to relate; to tell

ha'iolelo - a speech

ha'i olelo - to make a speech

haole - a white person (ivory colored skin)

hau'oli - to be happy; to be merry; to be joyful; to rejoice

hauma-na - pupil: student
mau hauma-na - pupils; students
na hauma-na - pupils; students

halawai - to meet

halawai - a meeting

Hale - Harry

hale - building, house

hale kuai - store

hale kula - school, school building, school house

hale pule - church, house of prayer

hame - ham

hana - to do something; to make something; to work

hanai - to feed

Hanale' - Henry

haneli - hundred

hapa - half, portion
  me ka hapa - and a half

hapaiwa - ninth

hapaono - sixth

hapaumi - tenth; five cents; nickel

hapaha - fourth; quarter
  hapaha i hala - quarter past
  hapaha i hala o ka hola elua - quarter past two

hapakolu - third

hapalima - fifth

hapalua - half; half-dollar

hapawalu - eighth

Hawaii - Hawaiian

he - a, an

he - a declarative word

he ole - zero

he hele au - I go. I walk

he ... au - I am a/an ...

he ... oe - you are a/an ...

he ... oia - he/she is a/an ...

he ... oiala - he/she (over there) is a/an ...

he ... oinei - he/she (over here) is a/an ...

he mau - some

he mau ... oukou - you (more than two) are ...

he mau ... olua - you (two) are ...

he mau ... kaua - we (you and I) are ...

he mau ... kakou - we (you, they and I) are ...

he mau ... laua - they (two) are ...

he mau ... laua ala - they (two over there) are ...

he mau ... laua nei - they (two over here) are ...

he mau ... lakou - they (more than two) are ...

he mau ... lakou ala - they (more than two over there) are ...

he mau ... lakou nei - they (more than two over here) are ...

he mau ... maua - we (he/she and I) are ...

he mau ... makou - we (they and I) are ...

he po'e - some, some people

he po'e ... oukou - you (more than two) are ...

he po'e ... kakou - we (you, they and I) are ...

he po'e ... lakou - they (more than two) are ...

he po'e ... lakou ala - they (more than two over there) are ...

he po'e ... lakou nei - they (more than two over here) are ...

he po'e ... makou - we (they and I) are ...

hea? - where? which?
  ka mea hea? - which one?

heaha? - what? what is?/what are?

hele - to go; to walk
  hele aku - to go away; to go that way; to walk away; to walk that way

hele like - to go together

hele mai - to come; come here; come on; to move this way

helu - to count

heluhelu - to read

heluhelu aku - to read that way; to read to them

heluhelu mai - to read this way; to read to me; to read to us

Heneli' - Henry (from Henri')

hiki - to be able to do

hiki - to arrive

hiki aku - to arrive that way; to arrive there

hiki mai - to arrive this way; to arrive here

hiku - seven

hila - heel

himeni - to sing
  e himeni kakou - let us sing

hipa - sheep

ho'a' - to light, as a fire or a lamp

hoaaloha - friend

ho'akaaka - to make someone laugh; to make people laugh

ho'apono - to approve, to accept, to justify

ho'ea - to arrive

ho'eha - to hurt someone; to cause pain

ho'emi - to decrease in number or size; to lessen; to reduce in size or price; to diminish

ho'i - to return to a place

ho'i aku - to go back, to go home

ho'i mai - to come back, to come home

ho'iliili - to accumulate, to save

ho'iho'i - to return something

ho'iho'i aku - to take back; to return something to someone over there

ho'iho'i mai - to bring back; to return something to me, to someone over here

ho'ike - to show, to exhibit, to make known

hoo - the causative prefix
    hooakaaka - to explain, to make clear
    hooala - to waken someone

hooia - to affirm; to assent; to admit; to confirm; to profess; to make evident; to acknowledge

hooia'i'o - to acknowledge; to verify to confirm; to substantiate; to testify; to attest; to prove; to profess; to make evident

hooili - to devise; to will; to bequeath or leave in a will

hoohau'oli - to make someone happy; to bring happiness or joy

hoohalike - to match; to make similar

hooholo - to run, as an engine; to sail, as a boat; to drive, as a car

hookau - to put on some designated place

hookahi - one

hookahi hapaha - one-fourth

hookahi hapa haneli - one-hundredth

hookahi hapalua - one-half

hoolako - to provide; to furnish or supply

hoolike - to make even; to divide equally

hoolohe - to listen

hoolohe aku - to listen to him

hoolohe mai - to listen to me

hoomaa - to accustom; to make one accustomed to; to practice

hoomaka'u - to scare or frighten

hoomakaukau - to make ready, to prepare

hoonee - to move someone or something

hoopaa - to fasten; to study

hoopaa naau - to learn well; to memorize; to study well

hoki - mule

hola- hour, time

hola ehia? - what time?

hola ehia keia? - what time is it?
    hola ehia ho'i - I don't know
    hola ehiku keia - it is seven o'clock
    hola eiwa paha - about nine o'clock

holo - to run

holo - to sail in a boat or ship; to ride in a car

holo aku - to run that way; to sail that way

holo mai - to run this way; to sail this way

holo - Hawaiian pronunciation of the English word "whole"

holo oko'a - whole

holoi - to wash

holoi lole - to wash clothes

holoholona - animal

hope - after, behind; last, late; back, rear

hopuna olelo - sentence

hua olelo - word

huika - wheat

huila - wheel

huila palala - wheel barrow

huipa - whip

ka - to make a net; to knit

ka - the (singular)

ka - possessive sign

ka iala - his/her/hers (over there)

ka ianei, kainei - his/her/hers (over here)

ka oukou - your (more than two)

ka olua - your (two)

ka ka wahine - the woman's

ka kaua - our (your and my)

ka kakou - our (your/his/her/their and my)

ka ke kaikamahine - the girl's

ka ke kanaka - the man's

ka Keoni - John's

ka laua - their (two)

ka laua ala - their (two over there)

ka laua nei - their (two over here)

ka lakou - their (more than two)

ka lakou ala - their (more than two over there)

ka lakou nei - their (more than two over here)

ka maua - our (her/his and my)

ka makou - our (his/her/their and my)

ka Mele - Mary's

ka Pekelo - Peter's

kaa - to roll, as a stone

kaa - car, carriage

kaa ahi - train

kaa okomopila - automobile

kaa uila - electric car

kaau - Hawaiian name for forty

kaikaina - younger brother of a boy; younger sister of a girl

kaikamahine - daughter; girl

kaikamahine Amelika - American girl

kaikamahine haole - white girl

kaikamahine hana - working girl

kaikamahine Hawaii - Hawaiian girl

kaikamahine Pelekane - English girl

kaikuaana - older brother of a boy; older sister of a girl

kaikuahine - sister of a boy

kaikunane - brother of a girl

kao - goat

ka'u - my

kau - your

kaua - we (you and I)

kauhale - home, house

kaula'i - to dry

kauka - Hawaiian pronunciation of the English word "doctor"

kaukani - Hawaiian pronunciation of the English word "thousand"

kauna - Hawaiian name for four

kahea - to call

kahea aku - to call to him/her (over there), or to someone other than the person speaking

kahea mai - to call to speaker or to someone near speaker

kahi - a comb

kahi - to comb; to shave; to press or rub with gentle motion

kahi - one

kaka' - duck

kaka - to rinse

ka'ka' - to chop, as wood

kakau - to write

kakini - dozen; stocking

kakou - we (you, he/she/they and I)

kala' - Hawaiian pronunciation of the English word "dollar;" money

kalaiwa - Hawaiian pronunciation of the English word "drive," as a car

kalaiwa kaa - driver of a car, chauffer

kalana - calendar

kalana - county

kalani - gallon

Kale - Charles, Charlie

Kalela - Clara

kali - to wait

kamaa - shoe, shoes

kamaaina - native born; old timer; resident; villager

kamalii - children

kamana' - Hawaiian pronunciation of the English word "carpenter"

kana - his/her

kanaiwa - ninety

kanaono - sixty

kanaha - forty

kanahakumaono - forty-six

kanahakumaha - forty-four

kanahakumahiku - forty-seven

kanahakumakahi - forty-one

kanahakumakolu - forty-three

kanahakumalima - forty-five

kanahakumalua - forty-two

kanahakumawalu - forty-eight

kanahakumamoalu - forty-eight

kanahiku - seventy

kanaka - man; person

kánaka - men

kanaka hana - laborer, worker, working man

kanaka kalaiwa kaa - chauffer

kanaka lawai'a - fisherman

kanaka mahiai - farmer

kanaka poa' - robber

kanake' - Hawaiian pronunciation of the English word "candy"

kanakolu - thirty
  ke kanakolu - thirtieth

kanakolukumaiwa - thirty-nine

kanakolukumaono - thirty-six

kanakolukumaha - thirty-four

kanakolukumahiku - thirty-seven

kanakolukumakahi - thirty-one

kanakolukumakolu - thirty-three

kanakolukumalima - thirty-five

kanakolukumalua - thirty-two

kanakolukumawalu - thirty-eight

kanakolukumamaiwa - thirty-nine

kanakolukumamaono - thirty-six

kanakolukumamaha - thirty-four

kanakolukumamahiku - thirty-seven

kanakolukumamakahi - thirty-one

kanakolukumamakolu - thirty-three

kanakolukumamalima - thirty-five

kanakolukumamalua - thirty-two

kanakolukumamawalu - thirty-eight

kanakolukumamoalu - thirty-eight

kanalima - fifty

kanawalu - eighty

kane - husband, male, man, (male) person

Kaniela - Daniel

kanu - to plant

Kapaki - Sabbath

kapu - cap; tub; taboo

Kawika - David
ke - the (singular)
ke - sign of the present tense
Keaka - Jack
keia - this
keia mau - these
keia po'e - these; these people
keiki - boy, child, son
keiki kane - boy, male child, son
Keoki - George
Keoni - John, Johnny
Kekemapa - December
kekona - second
kela' - that
kela - sailor; tailor
kela lole - tailor
kela' mau - those
kela moku - sailor
kela' po'e - those; those people
kelapona - telephone
kele - jelly
Kele - Jerry
Kelemania - Germany
Kemakemapa - September
kena' - that (near person addressed)
kena' mau - those (near person addressed)
kena' po'e - those, those people (near persons addressed)
kenakoa - senator
keneka - cent
kenikeni - ten cents; a dime
Kepani' - Japanese
ki - to shoot
ki - tea; key
kia - deer
kiaaina - governor
kiele - gardenia
kiule - Hawaiian pronunciation of the English word "jury"
kika' - Hawaiian pronunciation of

the English words "cigar" and "guitar"
kii - doll; picture
kii - to fetch
kii aku - to go and get
kii hoomana'o - statue; monument
kii mai - to come and get
Kimo - James, Jim, Jimmy
kinai - to put out, as a light or fire; to extinguish
kini - tin, zinc
kini - Hawaiian word for forty thousand
ko - possessive sign
ko - your
ko Ana - Ann's, Anna's
ko Ane - Annie's
ko Aukake - August's
ko iala - his/hers (over there)
ko ianei, ko inei - his/hers (over here)
ko Iokepa - Joseph's
ko oukou - your (more than two)
ko olua - your (two)
ko kaua - our (your and my)
ko kakou - our (your, his/her/their and my)
ko laua - their (two)
ko laua ala - their (two over there)
ko laua nei - their (two over here)
ko lakou - their (more than two)
ko lakou ala - their (more than two over there)
ko lakou nei - their (more than two over here)
ko maua - our (his/her and my)
ko Makaleka - Margaret's
ko makou - our (their and my)
ko Malia - Marie's, Maria's, Mary's
koi - to ask; to urge or compel; to invite; to ask a favor
ko'u - my

kou - your

koho - to vote

kokoke - almost, near, nearly

kokua - to assist, to help

kolohe - bad, naughty, dishonest, mischievous

kolu - three, third

komo - ring

komo - to enter; to wear; to put on, as a dress

kona - his/her

kopala' - shovel

Kristo - Christ

ku - to stand

kuai - to buy; to sell

kuai aku - to sell to him/her

kuai mai - to buy from him/her

kuaka - Hawaiian pronunciation of the English word "quart"

kuawa - Hawaiian pronunciation of the English word "guava"

kuene - waiter

ku'i - to pound, as poi; to punch someone

kuini - Hawaiian pronunciation of the English word "queen"

kuu - my

kuka - coat

kukui - lamp, light

kukulu - to build, as a house

kula - Hawaiian pronunciation of the English words "school" and "gold"

Kulia - Hawaiian pronunciation of the English name "Julia"

kumu apala - apple tree

kumukula - teacher, school teacher

kumulaau - tree

kumulau - female breeder

kupuna - ancestor, grandparent, forefather

kupuna kane - grandfather, grand-uncle

kupuna wahine - grandmother, grandaunt

la - day, sun

la apopo' - tomorrow

la hanau - birthday

la nui - holiday

La Pule - Sunday (lit. prayer day)

laiki - rice

laikini - license

lau - Hawaiian word for four hundred

lau - leaf

laua - they (two)

laua ala - they (two over there)

laua me - he/she and another

laua nei - they (two over here)

laka - to lock

laka - to be tame

lakou - they (more than two)

lakou ala - they (more than two over there)

lakou nei - they (more than two over here)

lalo - down

lapaki - rabbit

lawaia - fishing; to fish

lawe - to take

lawe aku - take away; take that way

lawe mai - bring

lehu - Hawaiian word for four hundred thousand (400,000); numerous; very many; abundance; the highest Hawaiian number

lehu - ashes

leka - Hawaiian pronunciation of the English word "letter"

lele - to fly

Lepeka - Rebecca

lepo - dirt, dust, soil

liilii - little, small

lio - horse

lima - five, fifth

lima - hand

loa - length; long; too

loa - most

loaa - to be found; to receive; to acquire

lohe - to hear

lole - dress

Lopaka - Robert

lua - two, second

lua - hole

luahine - old woman

lua'hine - old women

luakini - church

Luka - Ruth

Lukia - Russia

Lukini - Russian

lumi - room

lumi aina - dining room

lumi hookipa - living room; reception room

lumi kuke - kitchen

lumi moe - bedroom

luna - up; above

luna - boss, employer, manager, foreman

ma - along, at, on, by

ma - (after name of person) and another; and others

maa - to be accustomed to; to become accustomed to

mai - (a directive) motion toward speaker

mai - negative word, emphatic mood

mai - from

mai hea mai? - from where? where from?

mai Maui mai - from Maui

maia - banana

maika'i - good, well

maika'i no - fine, good, well

maika'i no au - I am fine, I am well

mau - (plural sign) some

mau - always; constant; continual

maua - we (he/she and I)

maha'i - beside, next to

mahi'ai - to cultivate, to farm

mahope - after; later

Maka - Martha

maka - eye

maka - green, unripe

maka'ika'i - to go sightseeing

makaukau - to be ready

Makaleka - Margaret

makeke - market

makemake - desire, want, wish

makou - we (he/she/they and I)

makua - parent

ma'kua - parents

makuahine - aunt; mother

makuakane - uncle; father

Malaea - Maria

Malaki - March

malalo - under, underneath, beneath

Malia - Maria, Marie, Mary

Malia ma - Marie and another; Maria and others

Maliana - Marian, Mary Ann

malihini - guest, newcomer, stranger, tourist

maloko - in, inside, within

maluna - above, on, on top of, over

mamua - before

mana'o - thought, idea, opinion, theory; meaning, mind; desire, consider, suppose

mano - Hawaiian word for four thousand

mano' - shark

manako' - mango

manawa - time
  ia manawa - at that time
  i keia manawa - now

mane'o - itchy, itch; ticklish

Manuela - Manuel

mawaena - between

mawaena konu - in the center

mawaho - outside

me - with

mea ai - food; something to eat

mea oia'i'o - truth

mea kanu - plant

Mei - May

Meia - Mayor

Mele - Mary

mele - song

miliona - Hawaiian pronunciation of the English word "million"

minuke - minute

moa - chicken

moa kane - rooster

moa wahine - hen

moe - to sleep

moe - bed

moena - mat

mo'i' - king

mo'i' wahine - queen

moolelo - story

moopuna - grandchild

Moke - Moses

moku - to be cut

moku - ship, steamer, island

mokuahi - steamer

mokulele - airplane

mokuna - chapter, division, section

mua - first; front

na - the (plural)

na - for

na iala - his/hers, for him/her, belongs to him/her (over there)

na ianei, na inei - his/hers, for him/her, belongs to him/her (over here)

na oukou - yours/for you/belongs to you (more than two)

na olua - yours/for you/belongs to you (two)

na kaua - ours (yours and mine), for us/belongs to us (you and me)

na kakou - ours (yours, theirs and mine), for us/belongs to us (you, them and me)

na laua - theirs/for them (two)

na laua ala - theirs/for them, belongs to them (two over there)

na laua nei - theirs/for them, belongs to them (two over here)

na lakou - theirs/for them/belongs to them (more than two)

na lakou ala - theirs/for them/belongs to them (more than two over there)

na lakou nei - theirs/for them/belongs to them (more than two over here)

na maua - ours (his/hers and mine), for us/belongs to us (him/her and me)

na makou - ours (theirs and mine), for us/belongs to us (them and me)

na'u - mine, for me, belongs to me

nau - yours, for you, belongs to you

naha' - to be broken

nahu - to bite

naloale - to be lost

nana - his/hers, for him/her, belongs to him/her

nana' - to look, to look at

nana' aku - to look that way

nana' mai - to look this way

nee - to move one's self

nei - article of location, meaning here

niho - tooth, teeth

ninau - to ask a question

ninau aku - to ask him/her/them a question

ninau mai - to ask me a question

no - for

no ka mea - because

noi - to ask for something; to ask permission

no iala - his/hers, for him/her, belongs to him/her (over there)

no ianei, no inei - his/hers, for him/her, belongs to him/her (over here)

no oukou - yours, for you, belongs to you (more than two)

no olua - yours, for you, belongs to you (two)

no kaua - ours (yours and mine), for us/belongs to us (you and me)

no kakou - ours (yours, theirs and mine), for us/belongs to us (you, them and me)

no laua - theirs, for them, belongs to them (two)

no laua ala - theirs, for them, belongs to them (two over there)

no laua nei - theirs, for them, belongs to them (two over here)

no lakou - theirs, for them, belongs to them (more than two)

no lakou ala - theirs, for them, belongs to them (more than two over there)

no lakou nei - theirs, for them, belongs to them (more than two over here)

no maua - ours (his/her and mine), for us/belongs to us (him/her and me)

no makou - ours (theirs and mine), for us/belongs to us (them and me)

no'u - mine, for me, belongs to me

nou - yours, for you, belongs to you

noho - to live, to reside; to sit; to stay

noho - chair, saddle
  noho lio - saddle

noho paipai - rocking chair

nona - his/hers, for him/her, belongs to him/her

nowela - novel

Nowemapa - November

nui - big, large

pa - fence

paa - to be fastened; to be secured; to be tight; to be completed; to be bound; to be learned

paa - a pair; a suit

paa kamaa - a pair of shoes

paa lole - a suit of clothes

paa naau - to be learned well; to be memorized

pae - landed ashore; to land ashore

paipu - pipe (for water)

pa-ka - park
  pa'ka - tobacco

pakaukau - table

Pake' - Chinese

pakeke - bucket; pocket

palaoa - bread, flour

Palani - France; French; Frank

palule - shirt

panako' - bank

pane - to answer

pane aku - answer him/her/them

pane mai - answer me

pani - to close; to shut

pani aku - close or shut that way

pani mai - close or shut this way

papale - hat

papale kapu - cap

pehea? - how?

pehea oe? - how are you?
a pehea oe? - and how are you?

Pekelo - Peter

Pelekane - Britain, British Isles, British; England, English

pelekikena - president

peni - pen

penikala - pencil

pepa - paper

pepe' - baby

Pepeluali - February

pii - to ascend, to climb, to go up

pii aku - to ascend that way; to climb up there; to go up there

pii mai - to ascend this way; to climb up here; to come up here

pio - to go out, as a light or a fire

pika - pitcher

piku - fig

pipi - beef, cattle, cow

pipi pulu - bull

piwa - fever

po - night
i ka po nei - last night
i keia po - tonight
i ka po apopo - tomorrow night

Po'aono - Saturday

Po'aha - Thursday

po'ahia? - what day? when?

Po'akahi - Monday

Po'akolu - Wednesday

Po'alima - Friday

Po'alua - Tuesday

po'e - plural sign; some, some people

po'e maka'ika'i - sightseers, visitors, tourists

poohiwi - shoulder

pooleka - stamp

poha' - to shine, as the sun; to burst, as a bubble

pokii - younger brothers or sisters

poli - bosom

popoki - cat

pua - flower

pu'a' - bunch

pu'a' - a herd

puuku' - treasurer

puka - door, hole

puka aniani - window

puka pa - gate

puke - book

puke a'o olelo - grammar

pule - to pray

pule - prayer

pule - week
keia pule - this week
keia pule a'e - next week
kela pule aku nei - last week

waa - boat, canoe

waapa' - boat, skiff

wai - water

Waioleka - Violet (name)

waioleka - violet (flower)

waiolina - violin

waiho - to leave something; to place something

waiwai - estate, property

waiwai - to be rich

waiwai - riches

wahileka - envelope

wahine - female, wife, woman

wa'hine - wives, women

wahine hana - working woman

wahine holoi lole - washer woman

waho - out; outer; outside
walaau - to talk, to speak
walu - eight, eighth
wehe - to open
wehe aku - open that way
wehe mai - open this way
weleweka - velvet
wilikina - nun; virgin
winika - vinegar

VOCABULARY

English - Hawaiian

A

a - he; i
about - ia; i
accept - apono, ho'apono
accumulate - ho'iliili
accumulation - iliili
acre - eka
agree - ae
all right! - oia!
America - Ameli'ka
American - Ameli'ka
an - he; i
and - a; ame'
and a half - me ka hapa
and with - ame'
Ann - Ana
Anna - Ana
Annie - Ane
apple - apala
approve - apono, ho'apono
April - Apeli'la
arrive - hiki, hiki mai; ho'ea
arrive here - hiki mai; ho'ea mai
arrive there - hiki aku; ho'ea aku
at - i; ia
at this time - i keia manawa
August - Aukake

B

backward - ihope
below - ilalo
berry - ohelo
better - oi a'e ka maika'i; oi aku ka maika'i

better than - oi a'e ka maka'i; oi aku ka maika'i
burn - ho'a'
    to be burning - a
but - aka'
building - hale
by - e
by - i; ia

C

church - hale pule
clock - uaki
come - hele mai
come back - ho'i mai
come here - hele mai
correct - pololei; pono
count - helu
cut - oki
    to be cut - moku

D

decrease - ho'emi
decreased - emi
derive - ili
    to be derived - ili
descend - iho
distinct - akaaka
do - e hana
do something - e hana
does - hana
does not have - aohe
dog - ilio
down - ilalo
downward - ilalo

drawer - ume
drink - inu

E

eat - e ai
eight - ewalu
eight-ninths - ewalu hapaiwa
eighteen - umikumamawalu, umi-kumamaoalu, umikumawalu
eighth - hapawalu
eighty - kanawalu
elevator - eleweka
eleven - umikumakahi, umikuma-makahi
Elizabeth - Elikapeka
Ellen - Elena

F

feed - hanai
fifteen - umikumalima, umikuma-malima
fifth - hapalima
fifty - kanalima
fire - ahi
fish - i'a
five - elima
five cents - hapaumi; elima keneka
five-eighths - elima hapawalu
five minutes - elima minuke
five minutes past one - elima minuke i hala o ka hola ekahi
five minutes to ten - elima minuke i koe kani ka hola umi
five-sixths - elima hapaono
for - na; no
forty - kanaha'
forward - imua
four - eha'
four-fifths - eha' hapalima
four hundred - eha' haneli

four-hundredths - eha' hapa haneli
four thousand - eha' kaukani
four thousandths - eha' hapa kau-kani
fourteen - umikumaha', umikuma-maha'
fourth - hapaha'
friend - hoaaloha

G

give - haawi, haawi aku, haawi mai
give him/her - haawi aku
give me - haawi mai
go - hele, hele aku
go away - hele aku
go down - iho aku
go together - hele like
gold - kula
greeting - aloha
greetings! - aloha!

H

half - hapa, hapalua
half-dollar - hapalua
ham - hame
happy - hauoli
Harry - Hale
has not - a'ohe
have not - a'ohe
Hawaiian - Hawaii
he - oia
he (over here) - oianei, oinei
he (over there) - oia ala, oiala
heap - iliili
heel - hila
Henry - Hanale', Heneli'
her - iaia
her - ana, ona, ka'na, kona
her (over here) - a ia nei, ainei,

iainei, o ia nei, oinei, ka inei, ko inei

her (over there) - a iala, iaiala, o iala, ka iala, ko iala

hers - ana, ona, nana, nona

hers - iaia

hers (over here) - a ianei, ainei

hers (over there) - a iala

him - ana, iaia, ona

him (over here) - a ianei, a inei, iainei, o ianei, oinei

him (over there) - a iala, iaiala, o iala

his - ana, ona, kana, kona

his (over here) - a ianei, a inei, o ianei, o inei

his (over there) - a iala, o iala

home - home; kauhale
   at home - i kauhale
   to the home of - i ka home o; i kahi o

house - hale

how do you do? - aloha!; aloha, ea!

how many - ehia

how old - ehia makahiki
   how old are you? - ehia ou makahiki?

hundred - haneli

hurt - eha
   to be hurt - eha
   to hurt someone - ho'eha

I

I - au; owau

I do not have - a'ohe a'u; a'ohe o'u

I have - he ... ka'u; he ... ko'u

I have a - he ... ka'u; he ... ko'u

I have no - a'ohe a'u; a'ohe o'u

if - ina'

in - i; iloko

in the midde - iwaena konu

in the midst - iwaena

ing (ending) - ana

inherited - ili

inherited by - i ili ia; i ili aku ia

ink - inika

into - iloko

Irish potato - uala kahiki

J

Jacob - Iakopa

January - Ianuali

Jesus - Iesu

John - Ioane; Keoni

Joseph - Iokepa

joyful - hau'oli

Juan - Ioane

July - Iulae

June - Iune

justify - apono, ho'apono

K

know - ike

knowledge - ike; naauao

L

lamp - ipukukui

language - olelo

large - nui

large quantity - iliili; nui

last night - i ka po nei

late at night - aumoe

laugh - akaaka

learn - a'o

leave - haalele; waiho

less - emi; emi mai

lessen - ho'emi

lesson - haawina

light - ipukukui; kukui
   to light (a lamp or fire) - ho'a'
   to be lighted - a
   lighted - a

little - uuku; liilii
  a little bit - iki
  a little less - uuku iki iho
  a little more - oi iki a'e
love - aloha

M

make someone laugh - ho'akaaka
make something - hana
match - ahi
match something - hoohalike
me, to me - ia'u
merry - hau'oli
meet - halawai; hui
  a meeting - halawai
mice - iole
middle - mawaena
midnight - aumoe
midst - iwaena
more - oi a'e; oi aku
mouse - iole
my - a'u, o'u; ka'u, ko'u
myself - ia'u iho

N

nickel - hapaumi
nine - eiwa
nine-tenths - eiwa hapaumi
nineteen - umikumaiwa, umiku-mamaiwa
ninth - ka iwa; hapa iwa
no - aole
noon - awakea
not - aole
now - i keia manawa

O

okay! - oia! pono!
October - Okakopa
of - a; o

of her - ana, ona
of her (over here) - a ia nei, ainei, o ia nei
of her (over there) - a ia ala, o ia ala
of him - ana, ona
of him (over here) - a ia nei, a ianei, ainei
of him (over there) - a ia ala, a iala
of them (more than two) - a lakou, o lakou
of them (more than two over here) - a lakou nei, o lakou nei
of them (more than two over there) - a lakou ala, o lakou ala
of them (two) - a laua, o laua
of them (two over here) - a laua nei, o laua nei
of them (two over there) - a laua ala, o laua ala
of us (him/her and me) - a maua, o maua
of us (them and me) - a makou, o makou
of us (you and me) - a kaua, o kaua
of us (you, him/her/them and me) - a kakou
Oh! - Auwe!
oh, dear! - auwe!
okay - oia
old man - elemakule
old men - elema'kule
one - akahi, ekahi, hookahi
or - a ... paha
orange - alani
our (his/her and my) - a maua, o maua
our (of them and me/their and my) - a makou, o makou
our (your and my) - a kaua, o kaua
our (your, his/her/their and my) - a kakou, o kakou
out - iwaho

outside - mawaho
outward - iwaho

P

page - aoao
pain - eha
path - ala; ala hele
perceive - ike
pile - iliili; paila
pipe (for water) - paipu
pipe (for smoking) - ipu paka
poor - ilihune
portion - hapa
pot - ipuhao
potato - uala
prettier - oi a'e ka u'i; oi aku ka u'i
  a little prettier - u'i iki a'e
pretty - u'i
proof - ka oia'i'o
pupil - hauma'na
  pupils - mau hauma'na; na hauma'na

Q

quarter - hapaha
quarter past two - hapaha i hala o
  ka hola elua
quarter to two - hapaha i koe kani
  ka hola elua

R

rabbit - iole lapaki; lapaki
rain - ua
rat - iole
read - heluhelu
  read to him - heluhelu aku
  read to me - heluhelu mai
recite - ha'i
  recite to him - ha'i aku
  recite to me - ha'i mai

rejoice - hau'oli; hoohau'oli
relate - ha'i
religion - ekalesia
road - ala; alanui

S

said - i; i oleloia
  said to him/her - i akula
  said to me - i maila
say - olelo
school - kula; hale kula
  at school - i ke kula
  to school - i ke kula
scissors - upa'
see - ike
  to see us (you and me) - e ike ia
  kaua
self - iho
seven - ehiku
seven-eighths - ehiku hapawalu
seventeen - umikumahiku, umikumamahiku
seventh - hapa hiku, ka hiku
she - oia
she (over here) - oianei, oinei
she (over there) - oia ala, oiala
sheep - hipa
side - aoao
sing - himeni
  let us sing - e himeni kakou
six - eono
six-sevenths - eono hapahiku
six-tenths - eono hapa umi
sixteen - umikumaono, umikumamaono
sixth - hapa ono, ke ono
slacken - ho'alu
small - uuku; liilii
some - i mau, mau
sore - eha
speak - olelo

speech - ha'i'olelo

steal - aihue

store - hale ku'ai

strawberry - ohelo

street - ala; alanui

student - hauma'na
    students - mau hauma'na; na hauma'na

sweet - momona; ono

T

tasty - ono

teach - a'o; e a'o

tell - ha'i; olelo
    tell him/her - ha'i aku; olelo aku
    tell me - ha'i mai; olelo mai

ten - umi

tenth - hapaumi; ka umi

their (more than two) - ka lakou, ko lakou

their (more than two over here) - ka lakou nei, ko lakou nei

their (more than two over there) - ka lakou ala, ko lakou ala

their (two) - ka laua, ko laua

their (two over here) - ka laua nei, ko laua nei

their (two over there) - ka laua ala, ko laua ala

them (more than two) - ia lakou

them (more than two over here) - ia lakou nei

them (more than two over there) - ia lakou ala

them (two) - ia laua

them (two over here) - ia laua nei

them (two over there) - ia laua ala

they (more than two) - lakou

they (more than two over here) - lakou nei

they (more than two over there) - lakou ala

they (two) - laua

they (two over here) - laua nei

they (two over there) - laua ala

third - hapakolu; ke kolu

thirteen - umikumakolu, umikumamakolu

this time - i keia manawa

three - ekolu

three-fourths - ekolu hapaha

time - manawa

to - a; a hiki i; i; ia

to be able - hiki

to be awake - ala

to be correct - pololei

to be cheap - emi

to be decreased - emi

to be hurt - eha

to be in pain - eha

to be less - emi

to be sore - eha

to decrease - ho'emi

to her - iaia

to her (over here) - iaia nei, iainei

to her (over there) - iaia ala; iaiala

to him - iaia

to him (over here) - iaia nei; iainei

to him (over there) - iaia ala; iaiala

to hurt someone - ho'eha

to lessen - ho'emi

to me - ia'u

to school - i ke kula

to see us (him/her and me) - e ike ia maua

to see us (you and me) - e ike ia kaua

to see us (you, him/her/them and me) - e ike ia kakou

to see us (them and me) - e ike ia makou

to them (more than two) - ia lakou

to them (more than two over here) -ia lakou nei

to them (more than two over there) - ia lakou ala

to them (two) - ia laua

to them (two over here) - ia laua nei

to them (two over there) - ia laua ala

to us (him/her and me) - ia maua

to us (you, him/her/them and me) - ia kakou

to us (them and me) - ia makou

to us (you and me) - ia kaua

to whom? - ia wai?

to you - ia oe

to you (more than two) - ia oukou

to you (two) - ia olua

tomorrow - apopo'; i ka la' apopo'

trail - ala; ala hele

true - oia'i'o

truth - oia'i'o

twelve - umikumalua, umikumamalua

twenty - iwakalua

twenty-eight - iwakaluakumamawalu, iwakaluakumamoalu, iwakaluakumawalu

twenty-five - iwakaluakumalima, iwakaluakumamalima

twenty-four - iwakaluakumaha, iwakaluakumamaha

twenty-nine - iwakaluakumaiwa, iwakaluakumamaiwa

twenty-one - iwakaluakumakahi, iwakaluakumamakahi

twenty-seven - iwakaluakumahiku, iwakaluakumamahiku

twenty-six - iwakaluakumaono, iwakaluakumamaono

twenty-three - iwakaluakumakolu, iwakaluakumamakolu

twenty-two - iwakaluakumalua, iwakaluakumamalua

two - elua

two-hundredths - elua hapahaneli

two-thirds - elua hapakolu

U

umbrella - mamalu

uncle - makuakane; makuakane ma ka hanauna

union - uniona; hui

until - a

up - iluna

upward - iluna

us (him/her and me) - ia maua

us (him/her/them and me) - ia makou

us (you and me) - ia kaua

us (you, him/her/them and me) - ia kakou

V

vested in - i ili ia

virgin - wilikina

vinegar - winika

W

walk - hele; hele wawae

Washington - Uakinakona

watch - uaki

watch over - kia'i

watch over - kiaʻi

we (he/she and I) - maua

we (they and I) - makou

we (you and I) - kaua

we (you, he/she/they and I) - kakou

where? - ihea?

where is/are? - aia ihea

where are you? - aia oe ihea?

where at? - aia ihea; ihea; mahea?

where did you go - ihea aku nei oe?

where have you been - ihea aku nei oe?

where is? - aia ihea? aihea?

where to? - ihea?

while - oia ai; oiai

white - keʻokeʻo

white person - haole

who? who is/are? - owai

whom? - owai?
  to whom - ia wai?

wick - uiki

William - Uilama, Uiliama

wire - uea

woman - wahine

women - wāhine

work - hana

Y

yard - ia' (pronounced eeh'-yah)

yes - ae

yes, greetings! ae, ke aloha no! (in answer to a greeting)

yesterday - i nehinei

you - oe

you (more than two) - oukou

you (two) - olua

young - opiopio

your - au, ou

your (more than two) - a oukou, o oukou

your (two) - a olua, o olua

yourself - ia oe iho

Z

zero - he ole, ole